HOW DID I GET HERE?

It's not a question of being lost,
but a question of being found.

Learning to Manage my Expectations
of God, Myself, and Others

Eboni Walker

Eboni Walker is an exceptional communicator with an ability to lead others into realms of understanding; with clarity and precision. This literary piece will help readers navigate the ebbs and flows of life while conquering the ever evolving mountain of expectations. *"How did I get here?"* You're about to find out!

- Pastor Levi Harrell
Best Selling Author & Strategist, Atlanta, GA.

We frequently hold grudges against others because they do not live up to our expectations. We, on the other hand, fail to match our expectations to their function in our lives. The author guided me through a series of thought-provoking stories and questions that forced me to look in the mirror rather than imposing my opinions and experiences on others.

- Dr. Jenny Thelwell
Amazon Best Selling Author, Miami, FL.

Eboni is a gifted writer and a dedicated servant of God who is passionate about making a positive impact in people's lives. Her genuine love for God and his people shines through in *"How Did I Get Here?"*, making it a powerful testimony of God's grace and transforming power. It's clear that Eboni's heart is set on seeing lives changed, and this book is a testament to her unwavering commitment to that mission.

- Pastor Melva Henderson
World Outreach Center, Milwaukee, WI.

HOW DID I GET HERE?
It's not a question of being lost, but a question of being found.

Eboni Walker

First paperback edition March 2023
First ebook edition March 2023
ISBN 978-1-7332907-5-3

Book cover and interior design by JohnEdgar.Design
Published by Revolutionary Diamond Publishing, LLC

This book is dedicated to my Trinity Tribe, my three exceptional children who pushed me to be a finisher, and my fantastic husband and number one fan. I love you all so much!

About Me
(Pre-Face)

We should never judge a book by its cover. It's natural for people to look at a person and see the result without thinking about the journey. In reflecting on the adversities and triumphs that have gotten me to this point, I don't remember much of my childhood. It's like pieces of my memory were erased, and I found myself in these latter years asking, "How did I get here?" However, a few significant milestones have pushed me along my journey right up to this moment.

I grew up around my grandfather, a Baptist preacher, who baptized me, helped me grow in my faith, and introduced me to the image of God at the tender age of five. Because of his strong beliefs, I grew up in the church. You know, inside the four walls of many buildings for Sunday service, mid-week services, choir rehearsals, revivals, you name it, I was there. Growing up in the church my entire childhood left me clueless about life outside church walls. As an adult, I spent most of my life trying to figure out how to balance church life with my everyday life. When in reality, they are one in the same.

Growing up on the west side of Atlanta and moving to the suburbs made me want to fit in with the suburban kids. I knew what it meant to be a "city kid" navigating downtown and riding Marta, but I found myself trying to define what it meant to be both a "church girl" and a "suburban girl." Being on the city's outskirts now opened my eyes to so much more. At this time in my life, I had only traveled on a plane once and didn't know much about people outside my city. It's like that city girl in a movie who moves to a small town in Alabama, and things seem gentler. It's a brand-new, slow-paced world, and I needed to be in the middle.

My family and life experiences trained me to be well-versed. I went to a predominantly black elementary school where I mostly fit in, a multicultural middle school where I had my first encounter with racism, and then to a predominantly black high school where I was teased for "talking white" and seemingly updateable because I was "wifey material." (We need to revisit this thought because you say you're a city girl, haven't seen much outside of your city, but then contradict yourself saying that you're "well versed") Even though being wifey material should have been a good thing, most guys my age were not ready for that. See, my grandmother taught me how to make biscuits from scratch and iron my grandfather's shirts; My mom made sure I knew how to cook the basics, keep a house clean and wash my clothes. But my faith community taught me the importance of prayer and worship.

I had all these skills under my belt, but I needed more guidance. Growing up, I experienced rough relationship dynamics but had strong family support. Some of my relationship issues stemmed from the lies I witnessed as a child. As an adult, reflecting on those relationship dynamics, it is alarming to see how many people around me did not live in their truth.

My family and the educators I had along the way were terrific teachers that contributed to my life, but I sometimes felt like I was missing the guide, the mentor I truly desired and needed. I now internalize the common saying, "It takes a village to raise a child," a little differently. The people we are connected to or associated with are just as important as those who raised us. Ms.

Lovelady from elementary school was one of those women who would give me the stare whenever I did something she disapproved of. She was the dance teacher for our Dancing Dolls group. She came to F.L. Stanton Elementary in the early 70s. She would select young ladies in kindergarten, and they would dance in her group until they completed fifth grade.

My mom attended the same school and always wanted to be selected for the group. She told me stories of how she would get upset when she was never selected. She called all the selected young ladies, and I thought, "My-oh-my, how we hold on to those childhood memories." Mrs. Lovelady was a significant person that helped me along my journey. She is one of the many women outside of my family that had an impact on the path I chose to take. It wasn't until I reached my high school years that I realized many of the educators I encountered had something in common. They were all members of a sisterhood that nurtured their growth, expanded their reach, and gave them the skills they needed to build personal and business relationships. I wanted to be a part of that movement. During my sophomore year in college, I jumped at the opportunity to become a Pearl of Divine Intervention. I put in the work and enjoyed making an impact in my community.

While earning my degree, I participated in many school activities and became the first attendant for the Alabama State University Queen.

Through some unforeseen circumstances, I could not pay for my final semester of school, which caused me to make the drastic decision to join the military. I covered the contract with tears. I truly understood what it meant to be between "a rock and a hard place." I had everything figured out and expected to graduate without any issues. Can you remember a moment when you felt this way? We all have a point in our lives where we thought we had it all figured out, but things changed. Certainly, life throws us curveballs, but we must continue to find a way through every adversity.

I wasn't 100% sure I was making the right decision to join the military, but I knew I had to do something quickly to finish school (in the time frame, society said that I should, but we will talk about that later). I cried on the way to the recruitment office. I cried while I was signing the contract. I cried in the car all the way back to my apartment. I was heartbroken that I felt I had no other way out of this situation. As He did throughout my life, God made beauty out of ashes (Isaiah 61:3, NLT). But this time, I felt He had abandoned me. I stayed in the military for eleven years, made lifelong friends, and gained skills I will use for the rest of my life. The military became a blessing in disguise. He didn't abandon me after all. It was a part of His plan. Isn't life funny like that? Sometimes what you think is a sacrifice actually becomes a blessing. I kept my faith, and it guided me through. Even in what felt like the middle of a storm, and when nothing made sense, God had it all worked out. It is hard to look outside our mess when we are in the thick of it all.

The military is where my journey with managing expectations began. Even though all soldiers had the same training, it did not mean that the training would make them good people. I found myself having to learn what to expect from these soldiers based on their past and not just their training. I always said if they were thieves before the uniform, now they are just thieves in uniform. People do not change based on the training they have had. People bring their beliefs into every aspect of their lives. They do not change just because of some training and a new outfit. It takes much more work than that.

We have expectations for people based on their position or who they are to us personally. We place this person or position on a pedestal because of the power associated with that position. Sometimes the person may not have asked to be thought so highly of, yet we hold them responsible for this standard even if they don't want to be. Honestly, it could not have been more apparent to me at that very moment that titles, positions, and socioeconomic status, are just that—a status. Neither one of those things can replace being a person first. Regardless of status, they are not exempt from a past or having struggles. Putting on the uniform does not change who they are; it changes their appearance. Therefore, I had to learn to manage my expectations of people in uniform. I had to remember that the uniform did not automatically make them good people. I made peace with the fact that my expectation was unrealistic on the pretense that they "should know" 'when they could not truly understand my needs.

So, this book is a deep dive into how I learned to manage my expectations throughout my life's journey, but most importantly, how you can start to do the same. At the end of each chapter, you'll find a scripture and prayer to help you navigate that area of expectations being in tune with your spirituality. Because let's face it, God is in the midst of all things, especially when we deliberately ask for assistance. Sit with these prayers and allow them to speak to you.

I'm excited to share my experiences and guide others through managing their expectations in life, understand the decisions that helped us arrive at where we are today, and understand how we arrived where we are.

Table of
Contents

Introduction:
What is Expectation Management?

Growing up, granddaddy used to always say, "Baby, don't worry about other people. You do what you're supposed to do." That was easy as a kid when all the fuss was about toys and games. However, as an adult, when I remember granddaddy's words, it doesn't feel that simple. Managing your expectations can seem unfair at times. It is challenging to understand people at the core of their being and not blame them for it. Managing expectations means you consider others' shortcomings by your standards due to how God created them and how they were raised. Wanting people to be and do as you have been and done is selfish. Let me explain what I mean.

I worked three jobs in college. I was a waitress at a restaurant, a department store manager, and a clothing company's customer representative. I worked hard. However, the waitresses would ask each other to cover a shift if they needed to be off for any reason. I would always help those who asked for coverage if I could. There was a time during final exam week I needed someone to cover my shift, and no one would offer to pick it up. I thought, "Wow, no one is going to help me after all the shifts I have picked up for them." The truth is that just because you work hard for someone else doesn't mean they will work hard for you. This was just one instance where I realized I needed to take charge of my expectations of others.

For years I have heard many people talk about the importance of managing expectations. However, I only understood what that meant once I had expectations to manage. Expectations come from your lived experiences, morals, perspectives, and values. How you manage those expectations also comes from your lived experiences. Your upbringing plays a significant role in the lens through which you manage your expectations. The negative or positive association we have with the word itself is the foundation for how we connect with or understand them.

"In expectation management, people take their instinctual need to disparage the ideas of others and use the technique consciously, regarding their ideas as they present them to other people." Now, what does that mean? All this means is that you can only place the weight of your perceptions on how a person thinks and expect them to function in that manner with the same knowledge or experience you have. It reminds me of an elder saying, "You'll know what I mean when you have kids." Some things only make sense to us once we have more experience.

Let's think about the relationship between the Apostle Paul and Timothy. The Apostle Paul wrote letters to Timothy while imprisoned in the Bible in the 1st and 2nd Timothy. The expectations of a person who is in prison will be different from those of someone who is considered to be free. In the letters, it is apparent that the Apostle Paul could manage the expectations of his environment because he was walking deeply in his faith. He used his time wisely to write letters to Timothy because he felt like he was his brother, and he wanted to make sure that he knew how to face or tackle the challenges of people or situations to come. He wanted to ensure that Timothy knew what to do, how to do it, and why he needed to do it. The Apostle Paul wanted to make sure that Timothy managed his expectations.

For example, the Apostle Paul tells Timothy in 1 Timothy 3:14-15, "Although I hope to come to you soon, I'm writing you these instructions so that, if I am delayed, you will know how people are to conduct themselves in God's household..." (NIV) and in

"Expectation management is one of the most powerful weapons in psychological warfare." How we perceive things in life is heavily connected to how we mentally and emotionally process information. This creates our perception, which is ultimately our reality. Our expectations of the nouns of this word (people, places, and things) should be managed to keep us from over-exerting ourselves mentally, physically, emotionally, financially, and spiritually. We naturally have expectations whether we want to have them or not. Even the person that says, "I do not expect anything" still expects because they expect nothing. Wanting something to happen at a specific time or a certain way is an expectation. However, for those that still think they have no expectations to manage, what does that say about that person's level of self-confidence? Remember that our thoughts and feelings link to our experiences and prior knowledge. Keep that in mind as you continue to read because you will see more about it in later chapters.

A MOMENT TO PONDER:

1. What does expectation management mean to you?

2. As you reflect, think about a situation in which you expected someone to react or reply to you in a certain way, but they didn't. How did that affect you?

3. How could you have managed that expectation so that it would not have a negative effect on you?

HOW DID I GET HERE?

I'm sure many of you, in the middle of both good and bad situations, have asked yourself, "how did I get here?" Things are happening and changing all around us. I'm adjusting in some areas of my life but not in others. People connect to me, but I am also losing people. Things continue to unravel, and it feels like I'm asking myself the same question over and over again: how did I get here? For me, a person that buries herself in her faith", I find that my spiritual mentor was right when she said that where I am now is the total of the decisions that I've made. Asking "how did I get here" is a rhetorical question because if I spend time navigating through decisions I've made. Through my actions, I can see why and how I got to where I am. In moments like these, I always remind myself of the power of my words and how my thoughts can cause me to stray off the path of excellence I want to operate.

This is why it's important to remember our assignment. We often want to focus on what I call the "nouns' of this world; the people, places, and things that may be positioned in our lives, but we need to remember to focus on 'the' assignment. The assignment is you! Before anyone and anything else, you are the assignment! Did I say it enough?

How are you handling the assignment? How are you completing the assignment? How are you treating the assignment? Is the assignment vital to you? Is the assignment at the top of your list? Is the assignment prioritized on your list? These are the types of questions you have to ask yourself about YOU. Part of the reason I wanted to write this book was to get out my thoughts and ideas about expectation management. But as I journey through the healing process of writing, I found myself asking specific questions over and over again. I wrote about my past and some things that got me to where I am today. The question still rang in the back of my mind how did I get here? So, as you navigate through managing your expectations in many areas of your life, the following question will still be, "how did I get here?"

How did you get there when you looked at your relationship with God? Look at your relationship with your spouse, children, or family members and ask, "how did I get here?" Then learning to manage your expectations of those people and situations will make all the difference in how you deal with people and situations moving forward. Though you are focused on understanding YOU, it's never a journey you should take alone. People will come along to make contributions that will help you reach your destination.

FRY-SIZED CONTRIBUTIONS:

On my life journey, I have encountered many people who have poured into me differently. I call these contributions "fry sized." Whether small, medium, or large, their contribution became the size of my expectation of them. Have you ever had that one aunt or uncle that gave you twenty dollars for every "A" you had on your report card? If they ever changed that twenty dollars to five dollars instead, you would've had a fit! That is why managing expectations is essential. However, learning about people and how they operate, and why they operate the way they do will help control what we expect from them. Once you get a deeper understanding, you realize that it was never about the twenty dollars, but more so, how that person was a giver and a motivator and wanted to ensure you stayed on the right path. You could depend on them to keep their word and do what they say. This is one way we, as humans, connect with people's morals and values. It is the realization that those significant elements identify who they are. Expectation management is just as you read it; learning to manage your expectations of people and situations based on your knowledge of who they are and where they come from.

As I sought purpose and understanding of myself, I became more mature in my relationship with God. Fasting, reading the bible, and praying gave me a deeper connection to God, which helped me learn more about myself. Doing this allowed me to gain a better understanding of people in general. I realized I had placed unattainable expectations on people and situations throughout my life. The magic that happens when we submit to growth, especially spiritually. God allows us to look within, but most importantly, He opens our eyes to view the world through His lens. I learned to look deeper into who people were and where they came from, essentially learning to give the benefit of the doubt. Although we are all different, we have many similarities. I understood why people behaved the way they did and why they communicated the way they did. God began to reveal the answers to questions I had always pondered. Why do people hurt each other? Why would a person want to break someone's heart? Why would someone hurt a child? Why are some people's hearts filled with so much hatred? Understanding the why gives clarity about who people are and where they come from and ultimately allows us to connect differently. Because I was intentional about connecting on a deeper level with God, He allowed me to communicate with people in a way where expectations do not play a role; instead, it manifests in how we interact. "We're born with an innate ability to communicate. We learn to communicate by listening to and watching other people; [practicing] and then adjusting how and what we communicate according to the response we receive" (Hasson, 2019, Introduction).

HOW DO YOU GET HERE?

All of this sounds great, but what do I do with it? How do I manage my expectations? We prepare to receive when we understand how we got where we are and focus on managing our expectations. I describe it as 'The meal of God.' You must be ready to eat if God is in a serving season. This is not a season to prep ingredients, but He has already put it together and is stirring the pot. He's ready to fix your plate, but are you prepared for your seat at the table? Have you done your part? This is why managing your expectations is so important. The information shared in this book is how God revealed that He is in the serving season. My obedience has made it so that I can share this word through a publication to make it so that we all can eat. Anytime God serves a meal, I can eat, you can eat, we can eat, but only if you've prepared. You don't have to have fake strength. Sometimes we look strong, but in actuality, we are weak. You can journey through this book as your true self and do the work to be who God has designed you to be for His kingdom.

STEP 1: Choose a specific time to read a portion of the book daily.

STEP 2: Use the notes section at the end of each chapter to jot down your thoughts as you read.

STEP 3: Be willing to try something different and put things into action.

Repeat after me: I am willing. I am obedient. I can do this.

Let's walk through this together.

xxx

Chapter 1:
The True You

This chapter is near and dear to my heart. I will uncover so many things from which I have no choice but to heal even as I write my story throughout this chapter. We all go through different seasons of how we think of ourselves. Feelings of unworthiness and lack of self-confidence were something I struggled with for some time. At one point, I remember saying things like, "I can't spell. I'm not that smart. I can't do that." I affirmed all of the wrong things. I planted negative seeds that grew branches and paralyzed my mental and emotional state. I carried this mental and emotional weight for years, knowing I would have to prune myself at some point. I knew I would have to cut the leaves, chop the branches, and eventually pull the roots of that which impeded me from becoming the best version of myself. I also knew that I couldn't do it alone.

For most of my life, I have had opportunities that connect with someone else. It wasn't until now that I realized none of my first jobs came only through my work. My first place of employment outside church summer camp was one that a friend helped me attain. I didn't get it on my own, but with the help of my best friend and someone she knew that worked in the four walls of metal, grease, fried foods, and burgers.

I'm not sure when I started looking for a job during my junior year of high school. All I remember is figuring out that the minimal amount of money my mom would give me was just not enough, and she did not have any more to give. I remember letting several people around me know that I was looking for work, and they always said, "Let me see what I can do." My best friend knew someone who worked at a local fast-food chain restaurant hiring, and the rest was history. This job was one of my favorites. I learned a lot about myself and about working with and for others. I realized that I enjoyed structure and organization, which played a significant role in my job following that. I didn't do it on my own.

Throughout my life, I realized that every opportunity I've had was due to a connection and/or my impeccable work ethic. When I realized that when I focus on who I am, the better elements within rise to the top. I function and do things with excellence. No matter what I do, I do it as if unto God.

THE PRICE IS HIGH

One of the things I say all the time is, "who's going to counsel the counselor?" Give and give to others, but sometimes the price you pay is to end up empty. Not protecting our space or energy can put us in a dangerous state of mind. I have seen this occur many times in my life. People take advantage of the things you can do for them but remember; they do what you allow. Sometimes we allow ourselves to be used, and we don't realize how much energy it takes from us. Something special within us attracts people; if they see it before you do, they may try to take advantage of it. I have found myself in this space and many others throughout my journey. I've learned many lessons, lost and gained, grieving and growing, yet continued to push through it all. I am a healer by nature. People seem to receive still even when I think I have nothing to give. Yet sometimes, I may feel broken or empty in this life, as if I have nothing to give. We must remember that we cannot heal everybody because we have a healing spirit. Relationship with the almighty is critical for discernment.

It reminds me of this story; it's a little long but bear with me...

So, one day, I left my last meeting and ran late to pick up my babies. There was so much traffic. My mind kept saying, "Lord, please let me make it on time because I do not want to pay extra childcare for tardiness." So even though I knew the way, I turned my GPS on just in case a quicker route came up. As I drove like a maniac, I was on the phone with a client closing a deal. As I made it to my side of town, I figured there were no more shortcuts, so I turned my GPS and proceeded to my destination. Now, since I was on the phone with a client, I was distracted, and though I thought I knew the way, my distraction caused me to make a wrong turn (stay with me). This made me more frustrated and caused me to have even less time to avoid any fees, or so I thought. I had to turn my GPS back on and find the quickest route to my kids because I only had 10 min left before I would have to pay.

My distraction (the client, conversation, chit-chat about biblical things even) caused me to change my intended path and have unnecessary frustration. I had clear directions (GPS) about how to reach my destination. Still, I could not focus on all the noise (conversation and GPS voice in the background), so I mistakenly eliminated the wrong noise.

SO, HERE'S THE LESSON:

Sometimes God gives us clear guidance about how to get to our destination. Still, we allow the distractions of life to make so much noise that we get frustrated and eliminate the wrong sound, not realizing that eventually, we will have to notice that we are off the path and have to turn the (GCG) God Clear Guidance sound back up (because it can't be turned off). My GCG helped me reach my destination with a few minutes to spare. Hallelujah!! Then God whispered, "if you just trust me, I will always lead you to your destination." Even when the talk is positive, it can be a distraction if it's not the conversation God intended for you at that moment.

A MOMENT TO PONDER: What kind of self-injurious statements have you made? How have they hindered your progress? How long have they kept you captive? These are essential questions to ask yourself to improve the expectations you have of yourself.

WE'VE ALL BEEN THERE

For some reason, it seems so much easier to focus on the negative. If you sit still now, I'm almost positive it would be easy for you to think of something negative that has happened to you today. Some people genuinely find it challenging to find the good in any day. Negative situations that happen to us in our lives sometimes leave us with a lot of baggage, but just because we carry those memories doesn't mean that we can't heal from them. The bible reminds readers repeatedly that God can use anyone, and guess what? He can use you too. Maybe you've heard of Paul. Paul was known as an eventual follower of Jesus. He spent the first portion of his life persecuting the early followers of Jesus in the region of Jerusalem and the latter portion of his life professing the gospel to anyone who would listen. God used him even though he was a murderer. God loved Paul even when Paul didn't love Him, and He does the same for us.

As important as it is to join together, we must remember that we are individuals first. To truly become one, a person must be whole. People like to say, "That's my better half." I understand what people mean when they say that; however, I don't quite agree with that comment. Each person should be whole and not half. I don't want a better half; I want someone complete.

As a marriage mentor, I know it is essential to growing together. My husband and I take pride in how we work in our relationship to ensure that we grow together and not apart. In this instance, we read a book about marriage by Francis Chan and his wife. What was most interesting about the book was how it highlighted the importance of healing yourself. I connected with it so much that I want to share this paragraph in particular:

"Do you catch yourself being guarded? You go into situations expecting the worst, so you can't be disappointed. People have let you down, and you refuse to be hurt again. You protect yourself from disappointment, but in the process, you have lost your ability to hope. God doesn't want His children to live this way. He wants us to beam with anticipation. He wants us to be confident and thrilled about our future in heaven. He wants us "boast in our hope" (Heb. 3:6). Don't allow the lies of the past to kill your joy over God's promises for the future. Celebrate heaven today. Though people will lie to us, God never will."

How many of us go into relationships feeling hopeless and bringing the baggage of past trauma? After reading this, I realized that I did all of these things. I was guarded with just about every person I encountered other than my family; honestly, I was protected by a few of them too. I claimed to have no expectations. I just knew everything would turn out worse, so why bother? These were all indications of my wavering relationship with God. I was firm in my faith when I was a part of the youth ministry, but as I transitioned to college, my focus became worry based as I tried to figure out how to survive in my new environment.

One of my most profound memories of this was in high school. There was a competition to see who could earn the most money on scholarships. It wasn't a real competition, but my classmates and I made a big deal by earning free money to attend school. The counselors would calculate the number of scholarship monies each student received for everyone to see. They would project the highest student earnings at the end of each month. I was grateful for knowledgeable counselors who helped us get fee waivers for specific colleges, and they would push us to work hard. Though I wasn't the top earner, I was proud to receive more money than I could dream of to go to school. I even received a full scholarship to Bowling University, but my mother told me it was too far away, and she could not get to me if something happened. I went back and forth with her, but she would not let me go. That "NO" lingered with me for a long time, and I vowed that if I ever had children, I would not limit them to my fears but allow them to soar in ways I never could as a child. We've all been there!

We grew up still holding grudges, and I knew I held on to this grudge for far too long. The rejection of my desires coming from my mother threw me into unknown territory. I did not know how to get her to understand that I was mature enough to decide for myself. I wanted to do something no one thought I would do, and I felt like she was taking that opportunity away from me. With all of the sense that I had (yes, that's sarcasm you're reading), I declined every scholarship I had been issued, and I joined the military instead. I wanted to decide for myself. That was smart, right? At that age, I thought I knew what I was doing. Boy was I wrong! I did not think that decision all the way through. After four months into my stint in the military, I wanted badly to go to college instead. However, at this point, I had no scholarships and had to find the cheapest college I could attend since I had to pay for school out of my pocket.

I stumbled upon a historically black college and university (HBCU) that fit my needs, and I was excited about starting my new journey. The first few months of college were physically draining.

I was sick all the time from living in the dorm. I went to the emergency room four or five times during my freshman year, trying to get my body used to my new living conditions. Once I settled in, I began to live the college experience truly. I enjoyed the campus and learned much about who I was. My experiences at Alabama State University gave me much insight into who I could become if I maximized this opportunity. I became involved in every way I could. I sang with the gospel choir Tribe of Judah and toured the country with them. I made the dean's list, joined ELITE models, and became a sorority member. I was so proud of myself.

As I reflected on having such an incredible college experience, I could not help but think about my mother. Why did she deny me the opportunity to attend college but was okay with me joining the military? Going away to college would put me far away, but I would have been learning and growing. Joining the military was unpredictable and came with many "what if," but my mom signed the papers. This would have been an excellent time to manage my expectations of her had I known how to do that. To do so, I would have to understand the mother-daughter dynamic in my family. I sat with my mom and grandmother to ask about their experiences growing up to see if I could work through any generational concerns.

As I listened to their life experiences about their relationship, I quickly realized that the word love was an assumption, not an action.

Growing up, my mother didn't say she loved me, but she could use that word with things. It showed me that the way we love people and the way we love things is different. The older I got; I was able to manage my expectations because I realized that my grandmother had done the same thing to her. I couldn't expect my mom to do something that her mother never did for her. My grandmother never verbally told her she loved her; she just assumed that she knew. Wow, who knew that not letting me attend Bowling Green would uncover so much history! Uncovering this truth helped me understand not only the importance of love in my life but also the importance of making my own decisions. It was essential for me to research, plan, and execute to manifest how I view love and how to make that vision a reality in my relationships moving forward. However, I needed to understand my past and learn to recognize the opportunities to make decisions that get me closer to my goals.

A MOMENT TO PONDER: What process do you have for ensuring you recognize your thoughts and feelings when making a decision?

I like to jog my brain, remember if I have witnessed a similar situation, and analyze that outcome. Talking to someone, journaling, and sometimes just talking aloud allow me to release the thoughts I hold hostage in my mind and heart. It is essential to learn from your experiences to understand others, but most importantly, to understand yourself and mend the relationships that otherwise could stay broken forever. We must ensure that we don't leave a relationship without truly understanding the pros and cons.

NAVIGATING FAILURE OR DISAPPOINTMENT

There is no way to address all the expectations we place on ourselves without acknowledging what effect those things have on our lives. When you go through all these situations in life, they can cause unpleasant emotions and even fear that can alter your daily routine (anxiety); They could also negatively affect how you feel, think or act (depression).

As a child, I witnessed my mother exhibiting these episodes that no one could define at the time. I just knew something wasn't right. I often found her in a corner weeping and rocking back and forth. I would try talking to her to see if she was okay, but she would never respond. These visions were something that I carried with me into adulthood, and though I could define what they were now, I still wanted to ask her about them. I finally did one day, but she said she didn't know what to call them but just felt that she needed to pull herself together somehow. She remembers the feeling of being overwhelmed. Now, as an adult and a mom of three, I fully understand how life could have her in such a debilitating state. I have had some of these moments myself. I love my children, and I know they are a blessing but having them enhanced the anxiety trait that I have been able to suppress for many years. Children will be children. They make noise, they cry, they make messes, and they make plenty of mistakes. This required more patience than I have ever had. I needed to take a break from being a mommy and commit time to myself. I used to tell my soldiers that if they don't take care of themselves, they can't take care of anyone else. I had to find ways to lessen my load and decrease my chances of diving headfirst into depression.

This made me face issues from my past, and I decided to go to therapy. But, since faith is my foundation, I also choose to rely on my faith to draw more positivity my way. This Through the Word devotion about anxiety helped me. It was so good I had to share it all. On day one, it shares,

"You have searched me, Lord,
and you know me"
Psalm 139:1

Stop there. That's huge. God knows you. He knows everything about you. He searches within you, and He still loves you. Verse 2:

"You know when I sit and when I rise; you perceive my thoughts from afar"
Psalm 139:2

Even when you feel alone in your thoughts, God knows. You are not alone. When you move, and when you stop, He is there. He hears you, he listens, and he cares. Verse 3:

"You discern my going out and my lying
down; you are familiar with all my ways.
Before a word is on my tongue, you, Lord,
know it completely"
Psalm 139:3-4

I love that. For those times when you feel like you can't express your feelings clearly, God understands your words even before you say them. Verse 5:

"You hem me in behind and before, and you
lay your hand upon me.
Such knowledge is too excellent for me,
too lofty for me to attain"
Psalm 139:5-6

This is so beautiful. David is the writer of this Psalm. He was no stranger to trouble and quite familiar with mixed emotions. But here, he sets himself in awe at God knowing him, knowing him deeply. And as he reflects on it, he says that God's knowledge of me is too incredible for me even to grasp.

So, the first six verses are all about being known. But the next six move to God's presence and the impossibility of escaping it. Verse 7:

"Where can I go from your spirit? Where can I flee from your presence? If I go up to the heavens, you are there; if I make my bed in the depths, you are there.If I rise on the wings of the dawn, if I settle on the far side of the sea, even there, your hand will guide me,your right hand will hold me fast. If I

say, 'Surely the darkness will hide me, and the light become night around me,'even the darkness will not be dark to you; the night will shine like the day, for darkness is as light to you."
Psalm 139:7-12

God is there no matter how far you run or where you hide away. God sees you, and He knows you. You may feel alone in the darkness, but God is with you. You need to know that. When your thoughts take you to a bad place, and your feelings toward others are not strictly Christian, you need to know that God can handle that. The best thing you can do is open up and get honest with

God. Tell him how you feel about it. (Anxiety Part 1, Day 3)

You need to know that God can handle it when your thoughts take you to a bad place, and your feelings toward others are not exactly favorable. The best thing you can do is open up and get honest with God. Tell him how you feel about it. David did exactly that, and God recorded those thoughts throughout the book of Psalms so that you could see you're not alone. You're not the only one who feels like that.

Now, that still doesn't make it right. The point here is not to validate your thoughts or vindicate your self-righteous attitude; it should help you process your thoughts and move forward. David can move on once he decides to trust God. Immediately after David's tirade of anger against the wicked, he stops.

"Search me, God, and know my heart; test me and know my anxious thoughts"
Psalm 139:23

That is powerful. David invites God to search for him and to know him. Notice that's precisely where we started in verse 1: "You have searched me, Lord, and you know me."

Is anxiety or worry a sin? I've heard many people say that it is. They explain that worrying is not trusting God -- and that's a sin. While I see the logic, it's a dangerous conclusion. First of all, it's a manufactured conclusion. The bible does not say it directly. Secondly, anxiety is a universal human emotion. We all experience it. While it can certainly get to unhealthy levels, even sin, it's also a very usual and human response to the pressures and stresses of the world.

WHAT TO REMEMBER:

1. God has a particular kind of love for you. The people of this world have no way of expressing anything close to the love of God. If you have been hurt, broken, ridiculed, or even laughed at, know that the love of God is healing. His love can mend anything because He is love. Romans 8:37 tells us we can do ANYTHING through Him because He loves us. So, know that God loves you, and with His love, you can do ANYTHING, and you can make it through ANYTHING!

2. There are two types of people -- the givers and the takers. The giver does whatever they can to make people happy and avoid anything that makes others unhappy, even if it sacrifices their happiness. The taker does whatever they need to do for their well-being. They avoid anything that makes them unhappy with no regard for others. We want to be in the middle, where the good ground and balance are.

STAY FOCUSED

In 2014 I was laid off. Throughout the years I was out of work, I would find myself being assigned by God to certain people. These were people I felt led to help, whether with their career, education, or just someone who needed a helping hand. In 2015 God assigned me to a close friend. We talked almost every day, and we were building each other up. There would be times when I would encourage her and other times when she would encourage me. We needed each other in that particular season. She was going through a life-changing situation, and she trusted me to guide her, share with her, and pray with her through that situation. In 2016, I still wasn't working, and God assigned me to a close family member. I didn't believe, at the time, that this would be a family member that God would call me to, but they needed me in that particular season. Of course, as usual, I did what God wanted me to do.

This season, I was working on hearing God's word and being obedient and diligent. I didn't have the busyness of a corporate job or speaking engagements to get in the way. I was available for the spirit to move through me as I worked solely on walking on purpose. I was in a season of spiritual work. I felt God was using me as His vessel to get through to His people. I felt obligated to do it, not only because I wanted to be obedient but because I felt it was my way of tithing when I didn't have money. I would tithe with my time, gifts, and talents and do as God so assigned. Every time I was done helping someone, I knew that God would show me who was next on my list. It started to become a habit, and I looked forward to who else I would be able to help. For a while, I did not hear God's voice. Many times, I sat in silence. During those times, I began to jog my memory and started to reflect on past struggles and hardships. It took me a while to figure out that God assigned me to myself. I didn't think I was up for the challenge because I was unprepared to face the pain I had buried so deeply. Many times, we lend ourselves to others and never focus on ourselves. We have normalized "running on E" instead of help-ing others with the water overflowing from our cups.

I try my best to surround myself with people that inspire and motivate as I do, but the words and care from others are nothing like the care we receive from God. The words of those around you or even the books you read can be filling, but there is nothing like Holy Spirit. I realized during this time I was filled but spiritually empty, and I think that in this particular season, God was trying to help me understand that He was there to fill me.

This was a challenging season because I had to take all the information, knowledge, prayer, and guidance I shared with everyone over the years and apply it to myself. It was easier said than done. I have found myself this season where I didn't pray or read the word of God as much. I didn't spend as much time with God as I needed to. I found myself mentally and emotionally strug-gling. Trying to get a grasp of who and who's I was.

Finally, one day Holy Spirit reminded me that people do what you require of them. And I had not required much of myself; I was going through the world lackadaisical. On that day, I went and got my physical bible, removed all social media from my phone, turned my TV on TBN, and sat in

God. I exposed myself to God's word and the feeling of God, and I felt who God is. I was commanding my body to worship God. I told my body, mind, and spirit that it had no choice but to submit to God! This is true for you also! You belong to the ultimate healer. You belong to Jehovah Jireh. You belong to the king of kings and the Lord of lords.

HEALING FROM THE PAST

To manage my expectations, I had to understand where I came from. I had to lay out my life and deal with the issues that had somehow hurt me or changed my trajectory. In searching for my truths, I understood that what I needed to become was not perfect but whole. I had to identify situations that may not have been beneficial but essential to avoid falling victim to the same unruly situations. Focusing on our emotional well-being and acknowledging our high expectations of ourselves allows total healing in the mind, body, and spirit. As I think about who has helped shape my life, I think of my grandfather, who was pivotal in my upbringing. I also think of my mother, who did her best as a single parent.

My mother had me when she was 20 years old. It may seem like an age in which she should be able to handle becoming responsible for another human being, but I was her second child. At the time of my birth, my brother was three years old. Now she had to care for two kids as a single parent. At the time, she struggled with naysayers because she was young, unmarried, and had children. To add insult to injury, two men fathered her children, and neither was present in our lives. I remember my father would pop in and out or call every once in a while, but he was only sometimes present. By age five, I started to inquire about him and wondered why he wasn't in my life. Where was he?

From time to time, between five and seven, he would call and tell me he was coming to pick me up. Oh, the joy! One of the little girls who longed for her daddy. I wanted to be a daddy's girl. I would sit in my grandmother's living room in my cute little outfits, lace socks, and shiny shoes, awaiting his arrival. He would even call and assure me he was on the way or just a few minutes away, yet he never showed up. It was on these days that my grandfather would show me some extra attention. He would sit with me and listen to my questions about why he would do this to me and why my father didn't want me. He lent me his shoulder to cry on. He knew I was heartbroken in those moments.

It was these moments that solidified what my relationship with my biological father would be like. He spent most of his years figuring out ways not to provide for me. It was always weird because I learned he had other children along the way. One time he came by, and although I can't remember how old I was, I still yearned for his time and attention. I wanted to know who my siblings were, and I even wanted to meet his wife. I thought it would be exciting, but it turned out to be very weird. My brain was telling me to behave as if they were my family also, but my heart could not behave as such. The people and my environment were unknown to me. I was in a new place, around new people. He had so many rules, and I was trying to figure out why he thought he could control me when he didn't even know me. I wish I had known how to manage my expectations back then. I expected him to be more lenient, loving, and careful with me because I felt he owed me.

The one thing that stood out to me from that time was how white my teeth were. He made me brush my teeth in the morning, between each meal, and at night before bed. A close second was all the interaction I experienced with members of his side of the family. I met my grandmother and aunt, who were sweet and kind and seemed like all-around good people. As I reflected on my way back home to Atlanta, I felt I had a good time overall and wondered when I'd visit again. However, he never sent for me again; honestly, I think I was okay with that.

From that point forward, he began to pay child support, and that's the last I knew of him. My mom always let me know when she had received the money, and she would tell me what she used it for. She didn't have to do that, but she did so that I would know he was sending some money for my support. As a mother of three now, I understand how much money, time, and effort it takes to raise and invest in a child. I know now that what I received for child support was insufficient to support any child financially.

My mother eventually moved on and met someone she felt she could spend the rest of her life with. They dated for a while and decided to co-inhabit in our home. I thought he was a pretty cool guy until he got drunk or angry. Shortly after that, my mom got pregnant, and my little sister was born. The display of his anger became more frequent, and he started to beat my mother even when we were in the room. I was so sad when she got pregnant because I was afraid of what would happen. One night hearing them argue and fight, I could hear my mom's body slammed against the wall. I could hear things flying all over the room and hitting the floor. I got so scared that I rushed into the room only to see my stepfather on top of my pregnant mother, strangling her! He was sitting on her belly with both hands around her throat. I was five or six. What could I do to this man? I ran, jumped on his back, and tried to stop him from screaming and crying.

"Stop choking her!" I yelled as I saw that she could not breathe. I hit him in the face hoping to make a more significant impact and redirect his attention, but he snatched me by my shirt and threw me out of a two-story window. I was so scared I peed on myself. My body hit the window, the glass cracked, and I held on to the blinds. My mother found the strength to push him off and get to me. I was shaken to my core and will never forget that day, but little did I know it wouldn't be the most challenging day of my life.

Soon after that incident, my mom divorced that monster, and he moved out. I was so glad, but my mother was not the same person. She was so angry. She had to work all the time, raise three kids alone, living in the best place she could afford. Life was much more challenging for her now that there was only one income again. It was also a struggle for her to get after-school care now that she had to work longer hours. My siblings and I would go to our neighbor's house, and she would call us there to check on us. One day we went to our neighbor's house, but we didn't know their phone ringer was off, so every time she called, we had no idea the phone was ringing. Back then, people used landlines more than mobile phones. Around five or six that afternoon, she came banging on the neighbor's door and stormed into their house. She was so upset. "I've been calling you all, and no one answered! I thought something happened to you all, so I left work!" She was so mad. She took us home and whooped us like it was our fault. Trust me; we ensured they had their ringer on every time.

My mom had worked hard and gone through a lot of heartache, but she deserved to share her life with someone who would love her and treat her right. I can tell my stepfather broke her soul. It impacted us tremendously throughout that season of our lives. However, she started dating again, and eventually, she met a man from the islands that swept her off her feet. I don't know how they met. Somehow it seemed like he just showed up one day. Momma never let him meet us until she was sure he was the one. However, once he moved in, he implemented all of these rules. Later I learned he had a rough life growing up and had family issues that would later become more apparent. I knew those issues were serious when I saw him thumping my little sister in the mouth.

I thought to myself, "Who does that?" In my opinion, she was like five, and it was not an appropriate disciplinary action for a child. That was the first sign of abuse. Later on, he also abused my mother, and I knew then that he was not the person for her. Unfortunately, a woman in love is blind to others' advice. My whole life, I got in trouble for my mouth and speaking when I shouldn't be and saying things that I should not say. But after what he did at an event at my aunt's house, I knew I had to say something. I walked up to her and said, "you haven't had enough yet, have you?" She was pissed, as if any mother would be with her child speaking to her in that way. But I meant it. I was tired of seeing my mother beaten, thrown around, and abused because she didn't deserve it. She deserved better. And I wanted better for her, my brother, and my sister. He has stayed around for over 11 years to this day. Yes, you read that correctly, 'til this day. There has been some talking and healing to get to this point, but I still refer to him as my stepdad though they are no longer married.

When my mother met my stepdad, I didn't need or long for my biological father anymore. I felt he was filling in the gap, and the little girl within was somewhat fulfilled at having him as a male figure in my life. Though there was a lot of turmoil in our home, financially, he always made sure I had what I needed. Yet emotionally I had concluded that I would always be lacking. Abuse still ran rampant through my home, and many nights my brother, sister, and I would sit together and hold one another and cry while we heard our mother being beaten. It got so bad that we ended up calling the police on several occasions. My brother was the one who always wanted to stand up for my mother, and on his last encounter, my stepfather bashed my brother's head into the side of the wooden bedpost. I thought my brother was going to die. I was too afraid to do anything. I was frozen, and when I came to, I was in chaos in the middle of the room. The cries of my little sister finally made me recapacitate from this out-of-body experience. I grabbed my sister, took her down the stairs, and rushed out the front door. I jumped over the fence like a track star jumping a hurdle and banged on our neighbor's door for help. Unfortunately, there were many instances like this over the next several years. My brother decided to move out, and I felt abandoned and alone. My sister and I now had no one to defend us, and it could be over for us at any moment, just like it was almost for him.

In high school, things just continued to spiral down. It began to be more apparent why my brother left. There were occasions when I would get into arguments with my stepfather, knives and ripped clothing was involved, and the police officers had to be called. Most of my friends in high school never knew what I was going through at home except for those close to me. They'd joke around and tell others, "You never want to fight Eboni; she's never fought a female, only a grown man." I wasn't sure how to feel about that comment. I just knew that I was angry. I didn't deserve this treatment. I wanted to feel safe. I wanted my mother to step in and protect me. I knew she was going through her dilemmas, and so many times, I harbored these emotions from her. I now understand that it wasn't because she didn't want to but because she didn't know how to. I feel that for most of her life, she didn't know how to manage her expectations of people. For some reason, throughout her life journey, she didn't receive the respect or love that she deserved, and she started to think it was okay. Now, these are not her words. These are just the daughter of the abused words. Because in my mind, it couldn't be that she just didn't want to protect me. It was just because she couldn't.

In the middle of all of this going on, my biological father chooses to try to step in. He showed up at my house one day with his children, my brothers, and sisters that I did not know, and My stepdad was not too happy about it. He stayed a few minutes, and we could move past the initial shock. As time passed, my biological father's true colors began to show. He has a different faith base than I, and he believes women do not deserve as much power or authority as men. He once told me it was my responsibility as his daughter to maintain the relationship with him. What if I wanted to be connected to him that I needed to make sure I called him and reached out to him to help guide our relationship? This conversation infuriated me. I was so confused as to why he would place such a responsibility on me, the child who did not request to be in this world but was brought here by him, a man who had not chosen to accept responsibility for bringing me into this world. I could tell not much had changed.

LEARN HOW TO WIN

When I was a baby, I had Genu Varum, better known as bowlegs. I had a severe case of it, and my feet were turned inward. My grandfather made my mom take me to the doctor, and they had to put a brace on both feet. I remember seeing pictures of myself when I was younger with a bar going across my feet and my mom explaining how bad my legs and feet were. In the picture, I looked so happy and carefree. It just reminded me of how innocent we are as toddlers. I wish I could experience the same unfiltered happiness of those days. Yet, memories like those remind me that things could be much worse. There is a scripture that I have used in the signature of my email for the last ten years, and it reads,

> "For I know the plans I have for you,
> declares the Lord, plans to prosper you
> and not to harm you, plans to give
> you hope and a future"
> Jeremiah 29: 11

I've kept this scripture in my email to remind me that no matter how bad a day or situation may seem, God always has a plan for my life. He wants me to be hopeful. I knew that my life was just beginning, and this wouldn't be the only obstacle I would face.

SPEAK UP

As much as I talk now, would you believe I didn't speak until I was five? My mom said they tried everything, and I wouldn't say anything. She took me to different doctors, and they all said, "she will talk when she's ready. There's nothing wrong with her." They had no idea what would be released when I decided to talk. I started singing when I started talking. I just knew that my life's purpose was to showcase the vocal talent God had given me for the world to hear! And I did, in my way! It's one of the things that makes me proud the most. I traveled the states with a gospel choir and sang worldwide in the military. Sometimes we think acknowledging our accolades is a form of narcissism, but it's not. You can be proud of yourself. You can pat yourself on the back. Sometimes you may be the only one doing so, and that's okay. We must be able to uplift ourselves when no one or nothing else can.

In our darkest hours, the devil likes to play on our weaknesses. Why do we put so much emphasis and energy into what went wrong rather than what went right? We can't let the moments that didn't go the way we planned take over our minds. When you are feeling down and counting out, remember moments in your life that have made you happy. What makes you the proudest? What accomplishments, whether big or small, make you smile?

Although my insecurities tainted my experiences, I participated in many childhood events. Pageants, dance groups, and talent shows, to name a few. I pushed past the thoughts of "not being good enough" and put forth my best effort in everything I did. I didn't know what made me feel less than at the time, but now as I reflect, I realize it had a lot to do with the lack of relationship with my biological father. Knowing that he had more children and they got to live with them, and I didn't make me feel like he couldn't love me. I felt like I wasn't worth his time. If my father didn't want me, why would anyone else give me the time of day?

I did my best to push past these thoughts and always seemed to find the courage to participate. God's grace always ensured I came out on top in some way, even when I didn't realize it. Isn't that like God to always send a sweet victory to make you second guess what you believe about yourself? Ephesians 2:10 tells us that "we are His workmanship, created in Christ Jesus for His good works, which God prepared beforehand, that we should walk in Him" (ESV). He hand-crafted each of us, flaws and all. Even when we don't see the best in ourselves, He does. We must remind ourselves that God walks with us in everything we do, good and bad. It's tough because this is easier said than done.

I remember even when placing among the top performers. I would still compare myself to the contestants. In one particular contest, I lost to the most popular girl in school. She was so pretty. She had beautiful, silky hair that would curl up if water touched it. I remember thinking, "If I had hair like hers, I would've won." I didn't realize it then, but I was establishing a foundation of self-hatred. Moving forward, it was always something about myself that I wanted to change. I didn't want to wear my glasses. I hated them. I wanted the gap in the middle of my front teeth closed, but we couldn't afford braces. I could always find the bad when I looked in the mirror, and I was only a child.

HOW DO I KNOW?

There are many times when people can find themselves in a difficult place to navigate. It's like being in a dark space with an unforeseen beginning or end. In many cases, pulling yourself out of these types of scenarios can be challenging. I found it tough when you're in a situation where the stairs spiral down. Every step and thought takes you deeper and deeper into that dark place where depression can take over and end you. It seems, in these moments, that everything negative that could happen starts to happen. The downward spiral seems endless, and those negative thoughts start to take root and push people into despair. When people fall into that deep, dark place, it's hard to understand that we truly need to focus on who we are and whose we are. In these times, we need to manage our expectations of ourselves. But what does that mean?

To manage your expectations, you must dive deep into who you are and understand what you desire from yourself. How often do we find ourselves wondering what our true calling is? How do we find our calling, and how will we start walking in our purpose? How do we know what we are called to do? How do we identify our purpose and walk in it? These are questions that many people ask for the majority of their lives. Studies show that people who identify their purpose in life live longer. We want to do what we can to live the life intended for us and not cut it short. However, focusing on this can also apply unnecessary pressure and stress to our lives. To ease that pressure, it helps to identify our calling. Though this may seem like an easy thing to do, it is something that can take several years to identify. During that time of searching, here are a few things that can guide you toward understanding.

>*Pay attention to the things that move you. Whether emotionally or spiritually. For me, some of those things are altar calls, baptisms, praying for others, and moms and wives needing community. Now, what moves you?

>*Evaluate your self-talk. What are you saying to yourself? If it's not adding value to you, then change it. Write down some affirming words and put them everywhere. Find supporting scripture to speak to those tricky things in your life and put those up too.

>*Rest. Our bodies do some of their best work when we sleep.

>*Guard your gates. Be careful what you listen to and watch. Both have more of an effect on you than you know. Read your word. Listen to books. Fill yourself with wisdom.

WE ALL HAVE EXPECTATIONS

There is a lot of rhetoric around the concept that some people try not to have expectations and no real-life plan. "No expectations equal no disappointments." But that's not true. If you have some sort of want or need in a specific area of your life and desire for it to happen a certain way and at a particular time, that is an expectation. Sometimes we harbor so much hurt that we only depend on ourselves. We forget that God made us, and we need each other. After all, that is why we don't possess every single gift. Genesis 2:18 tells us that man was not meant to be alone, and that God created a helpmate. It's easy to say, "well, I'm just not going to expect anyone to help me. I'll do it all myself." The truth is, we cannot do it all, and God never meant it for us. We need each other! This is why it is so important to manage our expectations of others so we can make a conscious decision on the next step we need to take to move along and achieve our purpose. Think about a time your goal was prolonged or possibly not achieved because you waited on someone else. What do you think you could've done differently? We cannot manage the behaviors of others but can manage our own and how we react—managing your expectations will teach you how to WIN!

A different spectrum of "I'll do it myself" is when people change their plans and lower their expectations because they don't feel they can accomplish so much on their own. This closely relates to when people have relationships with others and don't want to be disappointed. Though strategies for managing expectations can be implemented in any relationship, a relatable experience is when a man or a woman decides that they want to be involved with someone. They may have "high expectations," and the person does not meet them. In this case, what would you do? Do you lower your expectations, or do you not get involved with that person?

Knowing yourself is the best way to be able to connect with others. Being in those relationships with close friends and families is a part of what makes us happy. "Close relationships in happiness are also tightly linked. Studies consistently find that people who have rewarding social and family relationships have higher overall happiness and satisfaction with life than those with less rewarding social and family ties" (Helliwell & Putman, 2004).

When things don't happen in your timing, it's okay. You have to trust God to guide you. Know that He will never leave you nor forsake you (Hebrews 13:5). You have to be in a position where you have forgiven yourself and others for what they have done to you throughout your life. You have to be okay with yourself enough to move on even if others who have hurt you do not apologize or admit their wrongdoing. I wrote these s statements just to remind myself that things will be okay:

- Some people never think they're wrong, and even if they figure out, they are, they will not apologize.

- Some people react inappropriately to the things you say because of their struggles, and they will not apologize.

- Some people have struggled privately, pretended not to struggle publicly for years, and don't know how to apologize.

- Some people have not forgiven themselves, so they can't forgive you or apologize.

Read the statements with power! Read them over and over again. Read them until you believe them. Read them until they make sense. Read them until they spark something within you that you don't desire to connect to anything or anyone that does not push you toward your purpose.

PRAYER:

Heavenly Father, thank you so much for loving me just as I am. You remind me in your word that no matter how far I may feel from you, you always keep me close. No matter what I've done, you still come looking for me. Even if the 99 are found, you will come looking for the one. So, Father, I thank you for reminding me that I am important to you, your child, and your authority. I can speak good over my life as you spoke good over the earth, and it will be so. Anxiety nor depression are my portions. They do not belong to me, but I know I belong to the Father. In your son, Jesus' name. Amen.

HOW DO I GET THERE?

ASK: What does it mean for me to manage my expectations? How did I find myself here?

BELIEVE: God loves me and wants the best for me.

CONFESS: I can do all things through Christ who strengthens me.

THOUGHTS: _____

_____

_____

_____

_____

_____

_____

_____

_____

Chapter 2
Relation-ship, Don't Drown

In. my upbringing, it seemed like all the adults in my family were happily married. Family gatherings always consisted of my aunts and uncles and their spouses. I observed that women always fix their husband's food. I grew up in the south, so traditionally, women always tended to the men, and the men would take out the trash, fix things around the house, and open jars with tight caps. It was like growing up in this fairytale land where everything seemed perfect. As I got older, I could see when someone wasn't having a "beautiful day in the neighborhood."

Seeing the men and women in my family work at their marriages initially scared me. I told myself I would never marry or have children in my early twenties. But it wasn't until God softened my heart that I saw marriage differently. Two people who love and care for one another and are willing to sacrifice in the way God desires to ensure their covenant does not break is what I wanted to emulate. Keeping this in mind made me very selective while dating in college. A young man I met and worked with on-campus later became my husband. As he tells it, I did not give him any play back then, but he gets all my attention now. After I said yes, we both knew we wanted to complete marriage counseling first.

It was one of the most challenging pre-marital things we did. My husband, fiancé at the time, didn't want to use a person we knew. But I had grown up around my youth pastor and convinced my husband that he was not biased toward me. We both learned this to be true during our sessions. He didn't cut us any slack. One of the most critical questions he asked us was to define the role we thought we should and would play in each other's lives. It helped us understand how we defined the role of a husband and wife and the history of why. We had to address the experience we had with marriage through our parents, family, and close friends. Looking at the pros and cons and then identifying what would work best for our marriage. He wanted to ensure that we were getting married for the right reasons and that we laid out our expectations for one another before we tied the knot. The pastor helped us lay out ground rules for our marriage and identify the non-negotiables.

I found it essential to make these adjustments before we got married. It was one of the things that I knew would help me know how to handle our marriage no matter what type of adversity we would face. I found that choosing to forgive ahead of time before any mistakes allowed me to choose that same forgiveness when it was needed. We agreed that divorce was a curse word and that we would be open to each other giving our 5%. The 5% Rule was a moment of truth. You could have no interruptions, and the other person was not allowed to respond with negativity.

When I said, "I do," I knew the ground rules we set would help us manage our expectations of the marriage. Yet, there is so much about marriage that people do not tell you, and these days it seems like marriage is just a trend.

When you marry a person, it's impossible to know everything about them. All you know is what they have shown you. Depending on how much time you have spent getting to know this person, all you see is the surface level of information. Depending on your foundational beliefs, you may or may not have lived with this person before marrying them. We learn who they are once we occupy the same space. When two people move in with one another, things may seem perfect at first, but at some point, disagreement may arise. Small things like how toilet paper should roll, how you should fold towels, and what belongs in the refrigerator. Big things like how late it is too late to hang out or how to spend money. How would you manage your expectations in those moments?

"In my married life, I and my wife have to remind ourselves many times that our faith in Jesus Christ is the centrality of the relationship. If I started to have faith in my wife more than Jesus, I depend completely on her for my strength and expect things from her that she might not be able to meet. But when I put my complete faith in the God who has called us to be together for a higher purpose, which is greater than our own lives, it enables us to support and help each other."

EVALUATE

Sometimes as women, we are complex. There, I said it! Seriously, sometimes we require things from others we don't ever require of ourselves. We want people to show us attention, and sometimes we want more than what we are willing to give. I'm sure that's a tough pill to swallow, but it's accurate for many women. In a relationship, sometimes we look for our spouse to fill our vacancies, and we shouldn't. Some things are our responsibility. I love these two quotes that help us better understand this:

> Marriage requires a radical commitment to love our spouses as they are while longing for them to become what they are not yet. Every marriage moves either toward enhancing one another's Glory or degrading each other.
>
> ~ Dan Allender and Tremper Longman III

> If you treat a man as he is, he will stay as he is. But if you treat him as if he were what he ought to be and could be, he will become a bigger and better man.
>
> ~Johann Wolfgang von Goethe

Sometimes we must ask God to fill us in all the ways our spouses cannot. We often place so much responsibility on our spouses to make us whole when we should be in God first. In marriage, there will be times when we may feel we need to include something or are dissatisfied with how our spouses complete specific tasks. It is a time for us to reach out to God the most so He can fill our needs. It's still crucial that we function in our roles and make time to spend with one another. We must communicate with our spouse if these things are not happening. Constantly evaluate the situation. If you feel that you are spending time with one another, but there is still a need, I challenge you to allow God to meet the need.

When we talk about the basic knowledge of being a wife, it doesn't mean that our definition of being a wife looks the same for everyone. However, the idea is to help people who desire to be married, are married, or are renewing their marriage to allow God to intervene.

To those of you who say, "oh, I do not desire to be married. I don't think that's necessarily my ministry or what God has designed for my life," not a problem. But do remember that God did not design us to be alone, and we have to make sure we're putting ourselves in a position to be open and receptive to whatever it is that God wants to do in our lives. I'm not saying every person has to be married, but I am saying that every person should be open to whatever it is that God has designed and aligned for their lives.

We can't be so close-minded with our spirit that when God desires to send the mate He designed for us, we can't even receive them because we've already decided it's not what God wants for us. Make sure that you are always open to whatever it is that God desires for you. Scriptures referencing not being alone:

Then the Lord God said, "It is not good that the man should be alone; I will make him a helper fit for him." NOTE: Notice one thing God is saying here: He will find and help mate for you. You shouldn't seek out that person but let God find the right fit for you. It also requires that you be approachable, but we will discuss that later in the book.
Genesis 2:18

"Whoever isolates himself seeks his desire; he breaks out against all sound judgment." NOTE: When all you hear is yourself, that can begin to become your truth. Don't just isolate yourself but be alone with God so you can use this time to grow.
Proverbs 18:1

Now for those who desire to be married, many of these things apply to you. During your waiting season, ensure that you prepare your best for the spouse seeking you out. To receive the blessings you desire, you have to be in a position to receive them. If you stay in the house, you will get an "in-the-house blessing." Some things God desires for your life can't find you because you are in pajamas and won't get out to put yourself in a position to meet people. Take yourself on a date, hang out with family and friends and enjoy life. Have a dynamic and interactive relationship with God and constantly seek Him out. Get involved with your church with your community, and continuously serve as He has shown us we should. Then everything that needs to find you will be able to locate you.

You may be engaged and preparing to embark on the journey of marriage and are unsure of some of the things you may encounter or how you may need to handle certain situations. I'll share some of the stories and strategies I used to tackle what most people call "marriage problems." The excitement of being in love and wedding planning can sometimes blindside people to the point that they may miss essential and meaningful conversations before getting married. If they are not careful, they can get sucked into physical attraction and the glamor of the wedding and not realize that it is a huge commitment. As you keep reading, you will find some strategies I share that will be important for you to look at before the wedding day, such as the importance of pre-marital counseling.

I want to create a safe space for people to understand that we do not have to repeat the cycle repeatedly. We can learn from each other by opening our eyes, ears, and hearts. I've made plenty of mistakes, we all have, but we can teach and learn from each other. Whether you have been married for years or are fresh on your journey, there's always something to learn. Marriage is a situation where we must constantly evaluate ourselves and be open to the fact that we are constantly evolving and must continuously learn to adjust. Once you are officially married, some say the title makes the relationship change. That is true to some extent.

Some of you may be on your last hope. You may feel like you've tried everything, and nothing is working for you. If you are reading this, you still have something within you that is pulling you toward finding your spouse and that you are willing to work for it.

HOW TO HANDLE DISAGREEMENTS

There is always a lot of nostalgia and fairy-tales when people imagine what their marriage can is like. Sometimes, many of those thoughts about marriage can be accurate, but some couples fail to understand that it comes at a price and requires sacrifice. Some people believe that when they marry their significant other, they will never get upset, frustrated, or have any disagreements. That is not true. We are human beings and will always go through emotions that sometimes won't be from happiness. We grow and transform into different versions of ourselves over time, and we must allow our spouse to adjust. One way to prepare yourself for times or seasons of change is to know that there is no perfect marriage. For years men and women have had differences that may cause them disagreements. Our make-up is simply different. The way we think, the way we behave, and the way we speak are entirely different due to how God orchestrated us. If you desire to thrive in your relationship, make time to learn about each other, specifically how to communicate appropriately. When your spouse makes you angry or upset, you must address those feelings and emotions immediately but appropriately. It is why when I take couples through pre-marital counseling, I ask them to make a list of things that make them angry and a list of things that the person does that makes them angry. This way, before getting married, you have an idea of whether or not these key points are things you are willing to tolerate or if they need to be addressed. Are any of the things written deal breakers? I realize that many people are blind by love during the beginning stages and may not think anger or frustrations will swivel their way into their marriage in any way but understanding what makes us angry puts us in a position to manage how we respond versus reacting to those triggers.

So, you read that correctly. Before you can address whatever, your spouse is doing that's making you upset, you have to address your issues first.

LOVE LANGUAGE

Gary Chapman, the author of The Five Love Languages, has excellent tools on his website that I utilize when counseling couples. He has three quizzes on love, apology, and anger that are very helpful when figuring out their stance in a particular situation. He walks you through statements you identify with most and then gives you results to review. These work even better if you have your spouse to take them so you can view the results together. Doing this task together will give both people a sense of responsibility and help them decide which areas to work on individually or collectively.

My husband and I have been through ups and downs in our marriage. We had a season when I was pregnant with our first child in which we struggled to understand how to make our marriage work. We were at a point where pretty much both of us were unhappy. I would go days without talking to or ignoring him, and he was just as good at doing the same. I considered my husband too sensitive because he always said I didn't know how to talk to him and that I treated him like a child. My mindset then was that if you act like a child, you deserve to be treated like a child. I realize now that I had not managed my expectations of who I expected him to be. Though he has a little brother, he grew up as an only child, and I believe that has a lot to do with his behavior. He has a severe case of "only child syndrome." This mythical syndrome focuses on the temperament, adaptation, and social and emotional abilities of children that grow up without a sibling. But of course, "Any stigma attached to only children could be labeled on any child."

He was accustomed to getting what he wanted when he wanted it and having all of the attention focused on him. The issue here is that I went through so much as a child. I vowed to give myself the attention I deserved, so we "bumped heads" in this area because we both desired control and required undivided attention. We had created a lifestyle as single people that focused on what only we desired. We didn't have to think about anyone else but ourselves. It became an issue as we needed help to satisfy others' needs. Communication was lost. He started looking for attention from other women and eventually began to have an emotional connection with a specific woman. One of the things that hurt me the most was finding out that he would tell her, "I love me some you," which was my favorite phrase he used with me. Every time he said it, there was a certain level of passion behind it. But I was wrong. I felt bamboozled. I was hurt even though he didn't sleep with these women. He would send "good morning" texts and communicate throughout the day. It didn't matter that I was sitting next to him. He denied it every time I asked him about it. However, everything that happens in the dark will reveal in the light. I, too, have had my struggles. Though I have never cheated on my husband, I have had inappropriate thoughts unbecoming of a wife. In God's eyes, this is just as wrong because we must be mindful of negative thoughts, as they can become actions if we are not careful to bind them.

This season of unhappiness in our marriage happened because we weren't fulfilling the image we had in our minds of marriage or each other. My husband blatantly told me he wasn't happy. My reply was one with conviction, "Go and be happy doing whatever you want. Don't stick around just because we are having a child. If you're not happy now, then you won't be happy once I have this child." All of this happened the same day we had a maternity shoot planned. We had to work past our anger and frustration in silence through imagery. We held my belly with our unborn daughter. We smiled and held hands. We kissed and touched in ways that we had not in several weeks. It was through the mandated physical touch that we remembered our connection. After the shoot, we decided to sit and talk because we struggled to communicate how we felt. I am so glad that we did. It was that culminating moment that changed the direction of our relationship for the better. We were angry with one another and didn't know how to navigate those emotions.

Awareness of the people, places, or things that trigger your anger is essential. Is it with loved ones? At work? What happens when you react angrily? Think about those feelings and how you express them. Are you expressing them negatively or positively? Another point of reference from Gary Chapman is the quiz on your apology language. Now, this is good for people to do and share with their spouse so that they may understand how to apologize or how they should approach you to talk through a situation. The five categories for Apology Language are:

- Accept responsibility

- Expressing Regret

- Make Restitution

- Genuinely Repent

- Request forgiveness

I confirmed through this quiz that I desire most for others to accept responsibility when they are wrong and that I want them to express regret. It helped me understand why we must examine ourselves and manage our expectations of others' behavior. Thankfully, people change and mature throughout the years, and taking these quizzes may help bring light to a marriage that may not be going so well. It was a blessing to us and an excellent place for my husband and me to start.

JUST SEE ME

An article by Dr. Seth Meyers discusses the crucial difference between men and women in relationships. He discusses our need to be acknowledged. He mentions the importance of how we want to be seen and how we want to be desired by our significant other. Paying attention to those little signs to make each other feel special. He further discusses how we want the world to view and desire us. Meyers also shares the need to be loved. As a believer, I know the importance of love. There is a particular way in which God loves us, and He desires us to love others.

And he said to him, "You shall love the Lord your God with all your heart and with all your soul and with all your mind." It is the great first commandment.
And a second is like it:
You shall love your neighbor as yourself."

Matthew 22:37-39 NIV

It talks about God's love and passion for us and reminds us that love is essential if God desires us to love Him. The second most important commandment that He requires us to do is to love our neighbor as we love ourselves. So, if we are in a marriage, do we not have that responsibility to love our spouse the way God desires us to love our neighbors? And not to mention scripture also tells the husband to love his wife just as God loves the church. I don't want to skip over this scripture because many people take it out of context.

[21]Honor Christ and put others first. [22]A wife should put her husband first, as she does the Lord. [23]A husband is the head of his wife, as Christ is the head and the Savior of the church, which is his own body. [24]Wives should always put their husbands first, as the church puts Christ first. [25]A husband should love his wife as much as Christ loved the church and gave his life for it. [26]He made the church holy by the power of his word, and he made it pure by washing it with water. [27]Christ did this, so he would have a glorious and holy church without faults, spots, wrinkles, or any other flaws. [28]In the same way, a husband should love his wife as much as he loves himself. A husband who loves his wife shows he loves himself. [29]None of us hate our own bodies. We provide for them and take good care of

them, just as Christ does for the church, [30]because we are each part of his body. [31]As the Scriptures say, "A man leaves his father and mother to get married, and he becomes like one person with his wife." [32]This is a great mystery, but I understand it to mean Christ and his church. [33]So, each husband should love his wife as much as he loves himself, and each wife should respect her husband.

Ephesians 5:21-33 CEV

These scriptures are essential because most people only want to address the "wives submit to your husband" part. But that is not the only thing God is saying here. These scriptures remind us that marriage is a covenant and that both people play a significant role. Submission to another person is often a concept that needs to be understood. It does not mean either person in the marriage becomes a doormat (CLASB- NLT). We should submit ourselves to God first, which makes it much easier for us to submit to others. I remind myself and couples I've worked with that submission is a form of power. It takes a lot of obedience to read what the word says and follow through in the way we should. You know, submitting to His word.

In a marriage, the husband and wife are called to submit to one another. It is usually not as much of an issue in homes where both people have a personal relationship with God and understands His principles and instruction. In Ephesians 5:25-30 Paul devotes just as much time to telling husbands to love their wives as he does to telling wives to submit to their husbands. He also clarifies how a man should love his wife by being:

- Willing to sacrifice everything for her.

- Making her well-being a priority.

- Caring for her as he cares for his own body (CLASB-NLT).

Just because something is not popular does not mean we get to discard it and submission is one of those things. If we start with submission at the top of our relationship with God, it spills over into every area of our lives.

All these elements play a significant role when you get upset, angry, or frustrated in your marriage. If you have chosen God to guide you, you must manage your expectations of the outcomes of your discussions and conversations with your spouse. Learn when and how to address specific issues with them to have an open dialogue that leads to collaboration, growth, and positive change in the marriage.

WHAT ABOUT MY PURPOSE?

Many people get married and lose themselves in the process. In most cases, women tend to be the ones that fall into this category. Being nurturers by nature, we often dive in, forgetting ourselves and our goals. On the other hand, husbands often get consumed with providing for and protecting the family. They have their own set of pressures that society can't deny. We must recognize that when we are in a covenant, we both have things that we deal with, but we also have to remember who we are as individuals and what God has proposed us to do on this earth. We have a purpose when we come together in these great covenants, and God orchestrates our marriage to do a sure thing. However, we must remember our assignments. God has predestined us to do amazing things here on this earth, and we should never lose sight of that.

Being in a relationship in which you feel you are giving that person your all can make it challenging to figure out how to fulfill your purpose while in your role. Being in covenant with your spouse should enhance your purpose. However, sometimes people find themselves asking, "What about me? What about my purpose? What about what I'm supposed to do?" We can get so consumed with being in the marriage, parenting, or working, that our purpose can sometimes get pushed to the side. Depending on your situation, you may allow your spouse to pursue their purpose and put your purpose on the back burner due to timing. There has to be some flexibility for spouses to maneuver with one another. There has to be a give-and-take spirit, which requires communication, reflection, and lots of planning on behalf of each person. It's essential to do that because there's a season for you to pursue all that you've been purposed to do but the following season, the roles may be reversed. There needs to be a plan to delineate how that looks.

During the pandemic, we saw many families change and many roles shift. There was an increase in fathers staying home with children, women in the workforce, and/or mothers and fathers who started working remotely. With so much change and transition, people can quickly lose sight of their God-given purpose. What is most important is to learn how to submit to the Father first and ask Him to direct our path so that we can fulfill the assignments He has for us despite any chaos. It is about the importance of being yourself and identifying who you are in your relationship. Not as an individual but as an entity of a partnership.

"Oneness in marriage does not mean losing your personality in the personality of the other. Instead, it means caring for your spouse as you care for yourself, learning to anticipate needs, helping the other person become all they can be" (NLT).

Now, these can happen at the same time as you continue to discover your purpose and assignment. There may be sometimes when you have to focus on one thing at a time, and that's okay. The truth is, we must understand that these things happen synonymously and are ever evolving. As we evolve and navigate different life challenges, we can't let things distract us from our destiny. All in all, to be good to your spouse, you must be good to yourself too.

About your purpose, have you identified it? Are you working on it? Do you understand it? One of the things that I had to identify for myself was what kind of gifts God gave me. I'm sure you realize it takes some work to figure out. What stands out when considering your spiritual, physical, and mental capabilities? One of the tools I used to identify a few of these things was a spiritual gift assessment. It helped me better understand my gifts and how I can put them in motion.

The Changed Women's Ministry puts it like this, "Each of us was born to fulfill a specific purpose in this world. Even though we might not choose to acknowledge it, or have it figured out yet, God designed every single person with an incredibly unique combination of gifts that He wants to use to grow His Church. Thankfully, God has placed clues in our hearts and, through the Holy Spirit, guides us to discover our purpose."

God puts gems throughout our path and gives us opportunities to strengthen different skills so that He can prepare us for our purpose. Every one of our life experiences makes us who we are. We must recognize the natural talents God has given us, the different opportunities we've had, and the skills we've acquired to reflect and use them for our purpose. Think about where you grew up, where you have traveled, and what you have learned, and then you will begin to understand how all of those experiences have affected your life. Isolated, these events or situations may seem irrelevant, but together, they're leading us in the direction of a meaningful life that glorifies God.

I do not doubt that God has given you skills, talents, intellect, financial means, status, or influence designed to expand the kingdom. The question is, how are you using them? Pastor Mike Todd has a sermon series entitled "Who's the Minister Here." The series was a great reminder that the responsibility of drawing people to the kingdom is not solely on the pastors and ministers, but it is also the responsibility of those of us who know the Father. So when we look at our purpose, we must include the fact that whatever gifts, talents, abilities, intellect, financial status, or influence we have are things that we should use to help advance the kingdom in the best ways possible. We can't wait on anyone else to do it; it starts with us. We must spend time with the Father to understand and ask Him to reveal how these things have helped prepare us for the purpose He has designed.

HE CAN USE YOU

I know it can be challenging to believe that God can use the pain of our past for good. However, we see many occasions in the Bible where God uses the darkest, most difficult situations in people's lives for His Glory. In Matthew 1:1-17, we learn about the ancestry of Jesus. Looking at all the people in his bloodline shows us that even Jesus comes from a past where people had less-than-desirable reputations, were very ordinary and were evil. Still, we must acknowledge that human failures or sins do not limit God's work in history, and He works through ordinary people just as God used all kinds of people to bring His son into the world. He uses all kinds today to accomplish His will, and God wants to use us (CLASB- NLT).

In Genesis 37-50, the story of Joseph was sold into slavery by his brothers, who hated him. He had a hard time catching a break. After being enslaved, his master's wife lied about him, and he ended up in jail. He faced overwhelming feelings of betrayal, rejection, and abandonment—but God was at work. Eventually, because of his seemingly hopeless circumstances, Joseph became Pharaoh's second in command with the power to save his family and all of Egypt from famine and death. Looking back, Joseph can acknowledge that God had never left him but was quietly orchestrating a miracle all along.

Like Joseph, we all may experience pain or heartache. Some of us even suffer unspeakable tragedy or inexcusable abuse. However, stories like this give us hope to find purpose in our pain with God.

WHAT DO WE NEED?

When we become adults, there seems to be a little confusion between needs and wants. As children, needs and wants are often intertwined, and our parents help us understand the necessary things versus those that could wait for later. Over the past few decades, we have experienced this microwave society where we believe everything should happen immediately, exactly how we want it, without thinking about the elements required for the results to be produced. As adults, you would assume that we know this is not how things work. However, interactions daily with others prove people don't understand that good things take time and work.

When we think about what we need and want from our spouse, we must first understand what they are and are not responsible for. We don't need our spouse to make us happy. We are responsible for our happiness. "We are responsible to each other, not for each other." We shouldn't take responsibility for one another's feelings. They are our own, and we must handle them ourselves. Couples must set limits on each spouse's destructive acts or attitudes.

When we are in a relationship with someone, how do we explain what we need from them versus what we want from them? Too often in relationships, we assume our spouse knows what we need. Or we assume we know what they need. But one of the best ways for a marriage to grow and strengthen positively is to understand what you need first so you can share that with your spouse. It is a great reason to attend pre-marital counseling. A good pre-marital session doesn't focus only on the marriage but the individuals getting married. When was the last time you asked yourself, "what do I need, or what does my spouse need?

If I had to describe how I want to be treated, I am like a flower or your favorite plant. I require water and sunlight. I require good soil. I'm a great seed waiting to be planted in good soil. I'm excited to sprout and bloom into the fantastic tree that produces good fruit. I want to grow roots and be grounded and steadfast. I want you to show me some attention and speak to me in a tone that reminds me how much you love me.

Many trees can grow without much attention but pruning makes you great. Seeds that traveled with the wind and just landed may find themselves growing in a place they don't belong. But given the time and attention, you will soon realize you are where you belong; the pruning to get rid of all the deadweight hurts, but it will clear your path.

These types of analogies remind me of the many parables that are in the Bible. Specifically, the gospels are collectively the books of Matthew, Mark, Luke, and John. In Luke 8:4-15, Jesus told a story in the form of a parable to a large crowd gathered from many towns to hear him: 5 "A farmer went out to plant his seed. As he scattered it across his field, some seed fell on a footpath, where it was stepped on, and the birds ate it. 6 Other seeds fell among rocks. It began to grow, but the plant soon wilted and died for lack of moisture. 7 Other seed fell among thorns that grew up with it and choked out the tender plants. 8 Still other seed fell on fertile soil. This seed grew and produced a crop that was a hundred times as much as had been planted!" When he said this, he said, "Anyone with ears to hear should listen and understand."

There's something important that we can't miss as we read to understand these scriptures. The farmer was doing his best to ensure the seed was planted in the right place. Inevitably, some of the seed would not end up in suitable soil, but the excellent soil would produce a good crop regardless of where the seed fell. When trying to understand what I need, I must ensure I'm in the right place mentally, physically, and emotionally. What we need can be heavily affected by where we are.

²⁴Here is another story Jesus told: The Kingdom of Heaven is like a farmer who planted a good seed in his field. ²⁵But that night, as the workers slept, his enemy planted weeds among the wheat, then slipped away. ²⁶When the crop began to grow and produce grain, the weeds also grew. ²⁷The farmer's workers went to him and said, 'Sir, the field where you planted that good seed is full of weeds! Where did they come from?' ²⁸"'An enemy has done this!' the farmer exclaimed. "'Should we pull out the weeds?' they asked. ²⁹"'No,' he replied, 'you'll uproot the wheat if you do. ³⁰Let both grow together until the harvest. Then I will tell the harvesters to sort out the weeds, tie them into bundles, and burn them, and to put the wheat in the barn.'"

Matthew 13:24-30 NIV

Sometimes, as we navigate through marriage, we allow outside elements to affect how we express our needs. When we allow these outside entities to latch on to us, they grow with us, and it takes a while for us to get rid of them. We can't remove them until we get into a specific space and place in the marriage. It is why our relationship with the Father is detrimental. We must develop to continue on our path to purpose and understand who we are to discern what we truly need. We have to be intentional; otherwise, we will get attached to things that we should have never exposed ourselves to in the first place. Growing with these thorns will be a challenge and add stress. However, removing them too quickly could ruin our growth. So, we must wait until we reach the harvest space to remove them properly. This way, what God has already created in us can push us forward with conviction. All we have to do is be steadfast in His word so that the marriage may flourish. Though the rain may come, and the sun may shine, it may not be enough, depending on the type of seed planted. It requires attention to ensure the right amount of everything you need. Many women desire this, but many men don't realize that this is what they require to grow.

In marriage, you have to be willing to nurture the seed. Yes, your spouse has parents, but in marriage, you both have to help in the continued growth of one another. Sharing in the growth process as you evolve with one another through the years will strengthen your marriage.

PRAYER:

Father, thank you for loving me no matter what I have done, said, or experienced in my past. My spouse and I desire to see one another walk in purpose. I know that you brought us together for a purpose. Father, I pray that as I move forward, I'll focus more on what you have purposed to make a more significant impact as a couple. I will not be distracted by my past, what "they" said or what the world says I should be. I will focus on what you have purposed for me to do. I'm grateful that I'll be able to use every experience, good or bad, to serve your kingdom. I will honor you in all that I do. I'm grateful to be able to serve you publicly and call you Father. In Jesus's name, Amen.

HOW DO I GET THERE?

ASK: What type of relationship do I have? What type of relationship do I desire?

BELIEVE: There is a purpose for my relationship.

CONFESS: My relationship is fruitful in all ways.

THOUGHTS: _____

_____

_____

_____

Chapter 3
Friends & Co-Workers

FRIEND-LATIONSHIPS

I know what you guys are thinking, "what in the world does that mean?" Sure, when you have a friend, you develop a friendship, but a friend-lationship is different. A friend-lationship is when you become so connected to a person that you begin to google whether a friend can also be a soulmate. You begin to include them in your future family plans. Have you ever done that? A person could develop this relationship with a man or a woman. It can be positive or negative, but you may still feel attached and, in some ways, unable to separate from this person. When you do have to detach yourself from this type of person, it's like grieving someone living. These types of friend-lationships could inhibit how you respond in certain situations and even affect your daily decisions.

The connections we develop with people we've allowed in our small circle can also affect us emotionally. In a friend-lationship, you may feel emotionally attached or connected to that person. However, over time you may be hesitant about sharing all of your truth because you care about them so much that you don't want to add extra "weight" or pressure to their situation. You may sacrifice for them that you wouldn't make for anyone else. These are examples of your experience in a relationship with a significant other. If an altercation calls the relationship to end, a person may mourn the loss of that connection just as they would when losing a spouse or partner. It may require closure before moving forward; sometimes, it may not even include the other person. Everyone has different seasons; we must recognize when each season is over and learn to move on. When the connection to any person is not required for our purpose, it may be time for us to move on. Everyone can't go where God is taking them, but it doesn't stop them from being a seed. God plants seeds along the way to clear our path. Honey, if you could see my face right now, my eyes are looking over my glasses to approve this message as a WORD! Amen? Amen! (I wish you had this tone more throughout the book)

Usually, friend-lationsips develop almost instantly, and the two people have shared their thoughts, ideas, and passion throughout their lives. My best friend and I have many years of friendship. It feels like an entire lifetime. I met her in a youth church service in 1996 when I moved to the suburban neighborhood. My family started attending a nearby church, which helped me have a safe space from my abusive home. I loved my youth group. We always had something going on which kept me from being home. As I walked through the church doors for the first time, I saw a pretty little girl. I automatically started comparing myself to her (I know, bad!) She was involved in the service but still so reserved. She kept to herself but was kind and seemed to speak to everyone. I knew I wanted to befriend her. I felt attached to her already just being in the same room.

We became friends, and just like I expected, she was so kind and engaging with others at church, school, and even her dance team. She was smart, did as well in school, and was heavily involved in the youth ministry at our church. She was a few years older than me, so naturally, I wanted to be around her and follow in her footsteps. She was sweet and had an overall pleasant aura about herself. She had this impact on people. It wasn't just me who gravitated toward her. My mom must have agreed because she would let me spend the night at her house. I spent many nights in her home to get away from mine. We got acquainted very fast, and we became like sisters. Sometimes my little sister would tag along too, but she didn't mind because she knew my sister was trying to get out of our house. We developed a bond that I felt would last an eternity.

The years went on, and we continued our friend-lationship, but she had to leave me. I was dreading it. Her senior year was on full-throttle, and conversations about college became more and more frequent. Finally, the day I dreaded came. She graduated and was on her way to college, away from me. I was devastated.

My best friend went off to college, and the inevitable occurred. We grew apart. Looking back now, as an adult, I know I should have been happy for her, but I disagreed with her leaving me back then. You see, I had an expectation of my friend—of my sister. This expectation included my not wanting her to leave me (which I never explained to her). She was my shining armor, and I felt she had left me, even if it was for her advancement.

As the years went by, we were not connecting as we had in the past. Over time we both got distracted from our friend-lationship and engaged with other people, and other situations and life was life-ing. We both got married in 2012, and of course, we were at each other's weddings, but something was different. I didn't know the person she was marrying, and I'm almost positive she didn't know the person I was marrying. I realize now that she chose me to be her maid of honor primarily out of obligation to our friend-lationship. Moving forward, this realization caused me to be more intentional about our connection and interaction.

On February 4, 2014, I sent an email to four people. This email read:

> You are receiving this email because I consider you extremely close to me. I am currently reading a book entitled "The People Factor" by Van Moody. In this book, there is a portion that says, "If you want to take the next step in getting to know yourself accurately, ask a few honest, trustworthy friends for their opinions about you."
>
> I have a few questions that I want you to answer about me. I want you to be honest and straightforward. Trust me, I'm a "big girl,"

God is taking me to a place where I need to evaluate myself and my friendships the way He has instructed me to. So please take your time and answer the questions below and respond when you get a chance:

1. What do you think are my best qualities?

2. What do you think are my most significant weaknesses?

3. Do you believe I consistently tell the truth?

4. How well do you think I know myself?

5. What do you think is my biggest deception about myself?

6. Can you depend on me in an emergency or crisis?

7. In what ways have I earned your respect?

8. Do you trust me?

9. What one thing do you think I could do to improve my life and my ability to relate to others?

10. Do I treat other people with honor and respect?

11. Do I have a good record of keeping my word and doing what I say I will do?

12. Do you believe I am open to constructive criticism and making personal adjustments when others speak the truth lovingly to me?

I look forward to reading your responses and doing my best to grow as a person and as your friend.

As I read through the response, it was a moment of personal growth. This season, I learned how my friend-lationships were holding up and how much my relationship with my best friend had changed. She responded to the questions by sharing that:

1. What do you think are my best qualities?

Your communication

2. What do you think are my most significant weaknesses?

(no answer)

3. Do you believe I consistently tell the truth?

I usually believe you when you tell me something, but if there is any doubt in my mind, you always provide clarity or just come out with the entire story if that makes sense.

4. How well do you think I know myself?

I think you know yourself pretty well. Of course, life situations can make us questions ourselves, and we all make mistakes, but as the strong woman in God you have grown to be, I believe you know who you are, and you are adding to the foundation, not trying to figure it out.

5. What do you think is my biggest deception about myself?

You made an interesting comment on the phone to me before the baby shower about how you did not understand why you were paying for your baby shower and how you thought others were supposed to pay for it. As I often do sometimes, I decided to be present on the phone, but my silent presence is often the best way to show you I care. I believe sometimes you invest in so many people and expect the same, even if it's indirectly. You've never been the tick-for-tack kind of person. I've seen you sow seeds into people, watering them, giving them sunlight, and re-seeding if necessary, and the labor has not always been offered in return.

6. Can you depend on me in an emergency or crisis?

I do believe you are dependable in an emergency.

7. In what ways have I earned your respect?

Your consistency and transparency

8. Do you trust me?

Yes, and there's no need to elaborate.

9. What one thing do you think I could do to improve my life and my ability to relate to others?

Since living apart in different states I have not had the chance to interact with you around others since being married and with a family to really speak on this but I will say that it's hard to try and relate to others, but you have a way about you that allows you to attract all different kinds of people regardless of whether you can relate to their story, life experiences, etc.

10. Do you think I treat other people with honor and respect?

I do!

11. Do I have a good record of keeping my word and doing what I say I will do?

Yes

12. Do you believe I am open to constructive criticism and making personal adjustments when others speak the truth lovingly to me?

Yes

After answering the questions, she continued to share this:

Good morning,

I just wanted to let you know that I am grateful you included me in this email. I hope that I answered your questions as you requested of me honestly and thoroughly. Friendship and family, as you know, "was" a struggle for me moving to TN, but a lot has changed within our relationship and in my life. God has also taken me to a place that required me to shift gears and relationships. In the decade + years we have known each other, some things never change in a good friend. I may not have all the answers to your questions, but that does not change the fact that I still see you as a best friend. I've answered these questions based on what we've experienced and talked about when I lived in Georgia, during your engagement, and before you went overseas. In my opinion, our relationship has drastically shifted, and priorities have changed for the better. I may have expressed this to you, but I've felt I did not pour much into your life as we got older. I felt I was present, but a silent presence was the way to show I cared. I thought I knew so much about your life; maybe you know little about mine or me. Granted, you've always asked about things with me, but a part of me thought if I did not hear you out, I would lose you as a friend, but that has nothing to do with anything you did. God has taught me that there is nothing wrong with taking an interest in others' needs, feelings, and opinions. It takes humility.

The baby shower made me realize that you have plenty of love, which warms my heart. At the same time, I did not know many people there, which made me think that maybe our season has ended. It brought tears to my eyes to even think this, and I haven't prayed about this, so I'm not sure if that is what God is telling me, but the feeling is there. We've encouraged and confided in each other for many years, and I want to help you grow, but if we have run our course, I am okay with what God has for us. You have a wonderful husband and beautiful child on the way, and regardless of my opinion or others, as long as you're obedient to God, you can't go wrong.

Love you,

My heart sank when I read the first sentence of her response. She didn't even think she would be considered a person close to me. But I knew this. I knew we had been drifting apart. I knew we had communicated less than we used to. However, I also knew that this friend-lationship was not seasonal. I knew that she was meant to be a part of my life. Since that email many years ago, our friendship has made a shift. We both acknowledged that we had grown and changed in many ways, but we wanted to be a part of each other's life.

Often, we find ourselves in these positions where we feel hurt, frustrated, or even irritated when friendships reach troublesome times. One of the most important things we can do is share how we feel. When things happen, we can't just hold on to them and hope the other person understands. We can't just "ghost" a person we've been in a friend-lationship with. Honestly, it almost seems cowardly if you can't go to someone you consider to be this type of friend when thighs happen that you have something to say but won't say it.

When we get to these points in the friendship and are challenged, this is an excellent place to decide if this is a relationship we need to continue or if it's time for us to transition into the next season. We both agreed that we wanted to stay connected and keep growing with one another over the years. However, if you find yourself getting to these challenging points in your connections with friends, it may be a sign that it's time to move on.

There have been other significant friendships that were a challenge for me when it came to Friend-lationship status. They brought out some other challenges. One in which I was reminded that if people are looking to be offended, they will be offended. You can't help someone bound by the traumas of their life and holding you to the exact unfortunate expectations that they've held everyone else to. No matter how often you tell them that you aren't like other people or that you've tried to explain that you want them to hurt them, they're always looking for a way to hurt or be offended. It can be very challenging because it may leave you exhausted trying to maintain the friendship when it's more than likely something you need to release. Allowing them space and opportunity to grow, heal or be however they need to be without you.

Another instance is how it can be challenging for some when you mix work and friendship. I've worked with a few friends, and most times, it works out okay, but there's been a few times where I did it. You must be sure to keep work and friendship separate and establish some boundaries around both of those environments. We will talk about this a little more soon.

The truth is, friend-lationships don't always go how we think they should. We may find ourselves in a position where we are hurt, frustrated, or overwhelmed by connections we have or create with people we encounter on our journey to understanding how to manage these friendships.

The other side of relationships is that we have to be mindful of people who want to use us or be attached to us because of the gifts and abilities that we carry within. Sometimes people can see God's spirit within you, and they know that you are a force to be reckoned with. People naturally want to be attached to greatness. That's okay as long as it doesn't come with jealousy. Some people will even see things you've never seen in yourself, so they want to attach themselves to your future. You have to be mindful of these people because sometimes they want to use you for their betterment and leave when they get what they want from you. That can make you feel broken or torn by the abrupt disconnection in the friendship.

Many people have been hurt because they were connected to the wrong people. They've been lied to and betrayed, damaging them emotionally and making them unable to trust others in the long run. I've been in this situation before when someone I thought was my friend allowed me to do business with them. As I shared before, friendship and business may not mix, but I thought this would be different. We agreed on compensation, and things took off. We even had a conversation about how to navigate things if they didn't work out financially. When the business started to decline in sales, the manager notified me, but I thought things were still okay. However, the friendship ended when the business ended, and I could not figure out if something I did caused our friendship to end. To this day, when I think about it, I don't know what happened. I cared for this person and considered our friendship and business before making certain decisions. This person was close to my family and my children. I don't understand why the friend-lationship ended the way it did. Either way, it's not something that I moved on from swiftly. At first, I wanted answers and kept trying to figure out what I did wrong. I would reach out, but there would be no proper response. I had to remind myself that everyone doesn't belong in every season of my life, and maybe this person couldn't go with me to the next level or vice versa.

Sometimes we suffer from guilt and regret due to the time we wasted. We can feel like we missed out on the best years of our lives with someone who never intended to do us any good. However, there are valuable life lessons that we were meant to learn in these situations. Therefore, do not guilt trip yourself into thinking you could've done something better or differently; what was supposed to happen did, and it all works together for your good. Every relationship requires investment in maintenance, and when we realize whether or not a person is worth investing in or maintaining. There is so much we can learn from situations like these.

Some friend-lationships build on a common bond. Maybe you and your friend share a common talent, met at an event, or are interested in the same things. Sometimes the bond is fear or loss of loved ones or an experience that has affected your lives similarly. These are friend-lationships built on what many people call trauma bonding. Maybe they lost someone, and you lost someone, and you connected. Talking through those issues and the aftermath of a traumatic situation can be healing, but it can strain the relationship if the healing is not occurring at the same pace for both people. When trauma bonding is the root of a relationship, some people often feel stuck or obligated to the person to see them through the healing process, which can cause some regret.

WORK-LATIONSHIPS

Do you have work friends? Whether you work a nine-to-five or own a business. I'm sure you've established a rapport with some people at work. Sure, some people are just there for a paycheck, but others may enjoy the job and connect with others. While working in the same environment, we create relationships with people that often helps work to be a tolerable place to be. These connections grow into something a little bit more over time. Work-lationships are not the same. Not regular friends, and they're not family, but they're people who work with you and create this environment that's comfortable for you to be in, a safe space outside of your usual tribe.

It doesn't mean you change who you are while at work. These are specific people or associates separate from those you communicate with regularly. It is easy to share family stories and connect because you see them daily. You then start to form a "work" family or tribe. Having a work tribe may not look the same for everyone. Work-lationships develop when you complete tasks together and have opportunities to bond. It reminds me of my relationship with my hair stylist before I started my locs. She was and still is like family. She had been doing my hair for over ten years. When I gave birth to my first child, she would come to my house to do my hair so I wouldn't have to leave the house after giving birth. She gave my hair extra attention and ensured it was still healthy and growing. I trusted her to try new hairstyles or whatever she was learning at the time on my hair because I was comfortable with her. Our work-lationship has grown so much over the past ten years that we have gotten to the point where we pray together, cry together, and laugh together about life's circumstances to the point that it was weird because we didn't talk to each other every day. I realized we didn't need to talk daily to know we had each other's back. We had developed a work-lationship into something more than an average connection. As you read this story, I'm sure you can relate to whatever the dynamic is with you, your barber, your hair stylist, or maybe even your nail tech. Whatever the connection is, it is a nostalgic feeling. The feeling makes you feel like, "these are my people."

I feel lucky to have developed that great relationship with my stylist. However, not all work-lationships are positive. Or maybe they start that way and transition into something you don't recognize. These connections don't always yield fantastic relationships with people at work. Having a work-lationship does not mean that everything is excellent. Some work-lationships can take away your positive energy and inner peace. In these situations, we must be intentional about our goals. Even in the workplace, you can't forget what's most important. If connections aren't happening with others, that's okay. Focus on doing your job well and focusing on the assignment that the Father gave you, and make that the number one priority. Negative work people and work environments can be draining and overwhelming. Remembering your purpose helps you understand why you are there and should help you press through and get the job done the way the Father desires for you too. Too often walk away from jobs or opportunities because we don't feel like it's where we belong. We forget that it's not about how we feel. It's about the assignment. We must ensure that we are using our skill set in whatever we do to manage our work in the way God entrusted us to do it. Manage these work-lationships in a way that best suits the Father's assignment for us.

Some of the things people say to or about us in the workplace can affect how we function at work. Some of these people may have insecurities or issues that they tend to deflect to others. We can't let their voice be louder than the voice of the Father, even in the workplace. Their voice could be one of the limitations in marking the personal boundaries they set for you. This voice may come from someone who stays within limited boundaries and doesn't fully step into a more fantastic realm of authority in the area God has called them to. Be steadfast and know that their voice and boundaries will not limit your abilities. Don't settle for living under the approval or expectation of anyone other than God. They cannot lift you; they can only bring you down.

WHAT ABOUT WORKING WITH CLIENTS?

Work-lationships also requires us to understand our role in the workplace. However, we are making, in most cases, valuable connections. It's essential to allow everyone to do their job in the workplace. When I work with my clients, it's my job to provide them with the facts, the best tools, and the resources to get their job done. But it's their job to extend whatever grace they need to their team. For example, if I see a discrepancy in a report or someone's late, it's my job to provide the facts that the person was late. However, it's my client's job to extend the grace if they desire to say hey. It's no big deal. It's not my place to extend my grace to someone when I need to utilize the grace of the person that covers them.

When I speak to someone on my client's team, I make sure to speak with my client first. That way, I'm speaking with the same gray my client would instead of utilizing the level of grace that I would try to extend to a person from my point of view.

PRAYER:

Father, I am grateful for the gift of friendship and the blessing of working with others. Help me remember that my friends and coworkers are imperfect, just as I am, and that they are doing their best. Grant me patience and understanding as I learn to manage my expectations of them and myself.

Help me to be generous with my friends and co-workers, extending to them the grace and mercy that You extend to me. May I always strive to maintain positive relationships and be mindful of my words and actions. May I hold no unforgiveness in my heart so I can live the lives You intended for me. I ask this in Your name. Amen.

HOW DO I GET THERE?

ASK: Does this friend-lationship add value to me? Am I adding value to it?

BELIEVE: The Father wants me to have thriving and fruitful connections.

CONFESS: I will work to cultivate the connections God desires for me.

THOUGHTS: _____

_____

_____

_____

_____

_____

_____

_____

_____

_____

_____

_____

_____

_____

_____

_____

_____

_____

_____

Chapter 4
The Family Tree

I grew up in a family that values connectedness and constantly shows support for each other. My family spends every holiday and some regular days just hanging out, barbecuing, talking, laughing, and enjoying life. My husband had a different upbringing. He was not used to sharing so much time with extended family. When we married, navigating the family was a little awkward for us. In a sense, I was sheltered in terms of having those families that didn't communicate or spend time together like mine. I remember one of the first times my husband came around my family. He saw that everyone was conversing, laughing, and mingling. He asked, "do they act like this all the time? Do you all get together all the time?" It was almost as if my family being together and enjoying themselves bothered him. I quickly realized that he wasn't used to what he was seeing. I have an extensive family, and when I say we get together, WE GET TOGETHER! It's a lot of us. We are loud in everything we do, whether talking, laughing, or dancing. My husband was so surprised at how inviting my family was to him and as time passed, being with my family became one of his favorite things.

NEVER ALONE

I am grateful that my grandfather got to meet my husband before he gained his wings. It meant so much to me for him to see what kind of man he was, and my grandfather got to see what kind of man I was going to marry. It was challenging navigating when my grandfather was transitioning to be with the lord. I was getting ready to deploy on military orders and, at the same time, new to being engaged and having this person in my life. Sometimes we try to navigate challenging seasons of our lives alone. For the first time, I had a partner to help me through this challenging situation.

My husband attended my grandfather's funeral with me. Most of it was a blur, but I remember him holding my hand, holding me, and walking me through the entire situation for the few days I was able to be home from deployment. He showed me the type of man he was during this time. He didn't say much, but he was present for me. He was showing me he was family. My grandfather was a huge family man, and I was heartbroken that he wasn't going to be able to marry me as he had done for everyone else in our family. However, I was very grateful to have my pastor of 13 years be the one to cover our union. One of the important things he did during our wedding ceremony was to ask my husband to pray. I knew my husband prayed, but I wasn't sure how comfortable he was praying in front of everyone. I'm so glad our ceremony was recorded. There have been plenty of days that I've gone back to listen to it because it was so powerful. He prayed over me, our marriage, and our purpose as a couple. There was not a dry eye in the room. I knew then that my grandfather would have been so proud of the person God sent for me. During the reception, my mom said, "We don't have any in-laws. Either you're in, or you're out." It was something that my grandfather always said. My mom did a great job carrying out his legacy. His morals and values, when it came down to family, were the essential tradition he could ever pass down.

TRADITIONS

Now hearing this story, you might think that my family is just a perfect little white picket fence, and everything is always well. That is not the case. But I am saying that we communicate and don't let the sun go down on our anger (Ephesians 4:26). We bend over backward for each other. In many cases, that can be a good thing, but sometimes, depending on the mental and emotional space one can be in, it can get overwhelming. We grew up constantly being around each other, celebrating every special event and supporting each other. As we grew older, the family's matriarch noticed it had become challenging to pull everyone together. Our family lives all over the United States, and on some holidays, people come home, but not all holidays due to their jobs and the distance. Therefore, we've had to learn to embrace the times and moments that we do have. On the bright side, we get to travel to see one another, and our children get exposed to other parts of the U., S. Taking part in old traditions and spending time with one another to create new ones.

It all boils down to this. No matter your relationship with your family, there is a level of expectation for that relationship. Learning to manage your expectations of your family members can be challenging. One of the things you may struggle with is not wanting to let your family down. You know that they expect you to do things a certain way or in a certain amount of time, and you find it challenging to let them know when things aren't going so well or when you need some help, but your pride gets in the way. That's how I ended up being homeless. I let my pride get in the way. There was no reason for me to live in my car while I was in college, but I never called anyone in my family to tell them that I was struggling. I knew they had such great expectations for me, and I just didn't want to let anyone down. I figured I could fix it on my own and get it all figured out. I was grateful for a friend who stepped in. It allowed me time to reflect and push my pride aside.

Everyone's family looks different. We have to learn how to navigate relationships on all levels. However, there's something about those close family relationships with parents and siblings. Even once we become parents learning how to train our children in a way they will understand.

SIBLINGS

About 20% of households have only one child. That means we are growing up in a home with at least one sibling. These siblings, in many cases, end up being our best friends. Though many siblings argue and get on each other's nerves when they are young most times, those relationships evolve into ones we cherish.

Growing up, I had my older brother and a younger sister. Yes, I am the middle child. We have a lot of really great memories, and of course, you read the previous chapters and know that we also have some undesirable ones. Though our connections when we were kids were challenging due to our constant state of crisis, the older we became, the closer we got. I remember my brother chasing us around the house making spraying noises, holding his finger out, pretending to have a spray can, and it would scare us every time. I mean, this is what brothers do, right? He played with us all the time to scare us, but he wouldn't let anyone else scare us. He always has been and still is our protector. I remember one of my cousins squeezing orange juice in my hair after we played around and got into a disagreement about something. My brother ran to where I was swinging! He was ready to fight my cousin because I was crying. The orange juice had gotten into my eyes, and they were burning like crazy. My brother was one of the first men to come to my rescue. I remember growing up, through high school and college, when my brother showed up. No matter how far away, he always ensured I was okay.

My relationship with my sister isn't much different. Growing up, I remember times when I covered her body with mine to protect her from my stepfather. When I would put my hands over her ears and rock back and forth, singing songs to keep her from hearing all of the fighting and arguing going on in the house, it's crazy when you can see the environment's effect on a person, and there's only so much you can do because you're a child. But I'm so grateful for my sister. When we were younger, being five years apart seemed like a lot of years, so there were many times that we didn't do things together. As adults, we are closer than we've ever been. She is the best auntie to my children and the best sister on this side of heaven. She does not say much, but when she does, it's powerful. She, too, does not play about me. Though I'm the one that's usually giving the advice, there's been plenty of times she stepped right in with exactly what I needed to hear to encourage me through hard times. She's shown up for me in so many ways through our adulthood, and it's been a blessing to grow and connect with her over the years.

RIDE OR DIE

I remember going through a tough breakup, and my siblings took a long trip to see me. They came to my rescue at a time in my life when I didn't know if I was coming or going. I don't even remember how I survived. I couldn't see myself, but they could. I let my pride get in the way and, as I shared, ended up homeless for a while. After they left, things continued to get ugly, but they continued to check on me. Their love gave me the strength to keep going.

Reflecting on moments like these reminds me of how simple things used to be when we were kids. Though we faced many challenges back then, we didn't know how much more difficult life can be as adults. As kids, we say things like, "I just want to be an adult" or "I'm ready to start working," when in reality, once we become adults, we realize that adulting just isn't as fun as we'd thought it'd be. We would probably give anything to go back to some of those golden days when we didn't have to worry about mortgages, car notes, or any of the responsibilities that come with being an adult.

I understand that every relationship isn't like the ones I've described. I know that there are people who struggle with the dynamics of relationships with their siblings and are still navigating those relationships as adults. The adversities we have faced often put a strain on how we would like to connect with our siblings. One of the stories that come to mind when I think about the importance of siblings is the story of David. Most people think about David, and they automatically think about Goliath and how he used his sling-shot to bring down this giant, but there are a few things that happened before he defied all odds and became king. The Bible revealed a little about his relationship with his brothers.

In 1 Samuel 17, David inquired about the battle with Goliath and the reward that was being offered to whoever fought and won. His oldest brother quickly set limitations, pointing David back to where he came from and accusing him of having little thoughts and selfish motives. David could have cowered or stepped back, thinking his brother was probably right. Instead, he turned away to someone else who would give the answer he was looking for and point him toward something greater than himself. One thing's for sure if you let other people make decisions for you, you may get off the path God has predestined for you. If you don't tell your story, someone else will tell it. If you don't set your boundaries, someone else will set them for you. It's vital as we navigate relationships concerning our siblings. Whether our siblings are doing great or facing hardship, we must set boundaries and adhere to them.

PARENTS

My mom was a single parent of three children. She was doing the best that she could while working several jobs. We spent a lot of time at our grandparent's house. Once we got old enough, we spent the majority of our time home alone in Westlake courts. It was a place my mom could call her own, and I could share a room with my brother before my little sister arrived. So many things from my childhood play a significant role in who I am today. My mom was never really the person that said I love you all the time. Growing up, it was not something I was used to hearing. As an adult, it's one of the reasons that I decided that I wanted to say, I love you all the time to my kids. I wanted to ensure they knew it and didn't have to wonder. My mom showed us love the best way she knew how.

Seeing my mother work 'til her feet blistered and still come home to fix us dinner made me want more out of life. Not having a father around, sharing a room with my brother, and being home alone have pushed me to think deeper, not just about my life's journey, but to manage my expectations of my mother, my biological father, and all other people who had a hand in raising me. As I shared, my relationship with my biological father was non-existent.

The older I got, the more I understood the importance of not allowing how he chose to live his life and his decisions to impact how I live my life and make decisions. My grandmother still asks me, "have you reached out to your dad? Have you talked to your dad?" I always remind her that the phone works both ways, and if he wants to talk to me, he could call me as well. Throughout my adulthood, he's done a better job reaching out and trying to connect with me, but unfortunately, the relationship isn't there. I'm grateful that God allowed me to forgive him several years ago, so there's no anger or hatred. However, my life continues whether he's in it or not.

My stepfather did the best he could by stepping in to raise us, but there was so much trauma from that experience that sometimes it outweighed the love he was trying to show. He brought his trauma into the relationship and tried to raise us from an unhealed place. The way his parents had treated him was all he knew, and he didn't have an accurate definition of love or respect. So, when he tried to show our love, it was through material things, but he was so physically and mentally abusive that it didn't matter.

When raised by parents with a challenging past, it can be difficult for them to know how to raise their own children. The truth is, we should strive to be better than our parents, and well, that's subjective. Some people have struggled all their lives and live solely to overcome. How my mother raised us strengthened my ability to overcome specific challenges as an adult. I had to acknowledge that my mother did the best she could with what she had. Who she was mentally, physically, emotionally, financially, and spiritually had to be enough. She had no means of giving us more than what she had within her.

Sometimes I think we had these very unrealistic expectations for our parents. If you're considered a millennial like me, most of our parents are baby boomers or gen-x'ers. Many grew up in an environment where what we know now as bipolar disease, depression, and many other mental and emotional illnesses didn't even have a name. I am grateful to have learned so much through my childhood struggles and adulthood adversities. It has equipped me to handle situations differently than I have experienced with my children. I've learned how to separate things that I learned from my parents, both good and bad. I can decide what I will keep and discard to be the best parent I can be. I could use my experiences as my toolbox to help my children navigate life with fewer challenges than past generations. If I allow the challenges I faced as a child to get in the way of how I parent my current children, it would be a disservice to them. It is why I have had and still have a therapist to help me navigate different issues that may arise. This way, I can be the best version of myself for my children.

I'LL BE AROUND

We always expect our parents to be there for us. Even if they haven't in the past, as their offspring, we always hold on to a speckle of hope. Though they change as we grow, we must revisit those expectations as we mature. The things we expect as a child are not the same things we expect as adult children. My daughter told me that she expects me to take care of her and ensure she is fed and healthy. She also mentioned that she expects me to give her whatever she wants, but she laughed and said, "I know that's pushing it." We both laughed, but I was amazed that even at her young age, she realizes when an expectation is unrealistic.

Honestly, my daughter's response was similar to what I had in mind. But I believe there are different levels of guidance and support that I may or may not be able to provide. The way I guide my children is not the same way my mother guided me. However, if I were to guide a child the same way I guide an adult, the child may be unsuccessful due to my unrealistic expectations. I realize that, at times, I tend to place unnecessary expectations on my children and therefore create a revolving door of frustration, irritation, and annoyance that is detrimental to the relationship as it evolves. Issues from our past sometimes lead to some adult children not wanting to care for their parents.

Then he said, "You skillfully sidestep God's law in order to hold on to your own tradition. For instance, Moses gave you this law from God: 'Honor your father and mother, and 'Anyone who speaks disrespectfully of father or mother must be put to death.' But you say it is all right for people to say to their parents, 'Sorry, I can't help you. For I have vowed to give to God what I would have given to you. In this way, you let them disregard their needy parents. And so, you cancel the word of God in order to hand down your own tradition. And this is only one example among many others."
Mark 7:9-16 NLT

How many of us have said these exact words to our parents? What if we still received the same consequences as they did back then? As parents, we have a responsibility to manage our expectations of our children, but we must also manage our expectations of our parents. We can't expect them to give us or never learn what they don't have. We can't expect them to be someone that they are not. This is not an excuse for them, but this creates freedom for us to release any unforgiveness, frustration, or anger so we can live our lives in the best way possible.

WHAT TO EXPECT FROM CHILDREN

As a child, I was close to God. I remember having this unique relationship where I fully trusted God and knew He was protecting me. I went through experiences that could have shifted my thinking, yet they did not. Unfortunately, I was so good at hiding my pain that most people never knew what was happening. It was as if I was the protector like I wanted to make sure people didn't see the bad, didn't hear the negative. I wanted people to feel like everything was alright, even if it wasn't.

Years later, now a mother and a wife, I long for that closeness with God. As a child, it was much easier to accept God because of my inno-cence. I was open to receiving Him once exposed to who He is. It seems as if once we become adults, we learn and grow to understand things for our-selves. We tend not to believe in Him as much; we tend not to trust Him as much, and that causes us to have a more strained relationship with God. Therefore, we must be intentional about our re-lationship with God and not let life's distractions dictate our time with Him. It is why it's essential to point your kids in the right direction—when they're old, they won't be lost.

Point your kids in the right direction—when they're old they won't be lost.
Proverbs 22:6 MSG

WINNING SEED

Children are one of the most precious gifts a woman can bring into this world. As mothers, we are automatically connected with how this tiny seed, with so much speed, begins to grow and ma-ture from inside our womb. I remember listening to Dr. Cindy Trimm tell a fantastic story in one of her sermons about how, though we are born into sin, we are winners from birth. We are the winning seed. Many other sperm tried to infiltrate the egg first, but our seed won! What a beautiful way to see life, even from the beginning, no matter how you were conceived.

Mothers who are expecting many times begin reading books, articles, and blogs about pregnancy and birth. They watch YouTube videos, ask for advice, and buy every cute outfit they come across. They start wondering what this little human being will become, and we start developing what....? You guessed it. EXPECTATIONS! It's not much of a bad thing because, with this particular human, they can mold them into what they expect them to become. Selfish us!

As parents, again, we sometimes place unrealistic expectations on our children. Unfortunately, I am guilty of this. My husband and I have three children, and keeping them educated, entertained, and engaged every day is a task. I am teaching them to be kind, loving, and responsible people. My daughter is the oldest, and she is extremely intelligent. This little girl will converse with you, and you will forget she is a child. She is very hands-on and loves to do things herself. She knows how to prepare her meals; omelets, spaghetti, and pizza are her favorites. She is avid about making her favorite lunch at least twice a week, which consists of a peanut butter & jelly sandwich with a bag of chips and a juice box. Because she is so independent, sometimes I forget how old she is, so when she does something childish (because she is a child, lol). I fuss at her and then remind myself that she is only a child. I can't expect her to have the mental capacity of an adult, nor can I expect her to react or respond to situations in a manner that an adult would.

To manage your expectations of your children, or any child, you must first take into account the child's age. Secondly, think about their surroundings. Children behave according to who is around them and where they are. Please don't act like you don't know how they behave when their grandparents or family come around. Not to mention the way they respond in public places. In my household, when we are out and see other children misbehaving, I remind my children that we don't act like that because we are responsible for representing the Kingdom. We'll talk about this more later.

Some people think they can give you advice about raising a child when they never really raised a child themselves or, even better, raised them under different circumstances in a different era. Sometimes it's a millennial who has had the privilege of having help or even left the responsibility of raising that child to someone else. They may have provided child support but do not understand the day-to-day responsibility of raising a child. Until you have had the responsibility of being in the home, raising a child daily, your opinion of what I should do with my child is null and void.

In these instances, I like to provide inquiring minds this question: Have you taken the time to ask your child how the lack of you being present hurt them more than the money you provided each month? In most cases, they have not.

Those, of course, are my inner thoughts. However, the reality is that we all have expectations of how our children should behave or who they are to become. How do we train our minds to understand that regardless of what we expect of our children, they will do as they, please? How do we get out of our selfish ways of imposing our thoughts and beliefs on our children? Though the answers to these questions may not be easy, they are pretty simple. Parents must learn to become facilitators, guiding agents. Teach your children but allow them to have opinions and ask for explanations. Don't accept simple yes or no answers. Essential questions to ask your children as a facilitator are: Why? Have you researched it? Can you compare and contrast your response to mine?

Also, make sure they understand the importance of problem-solving. If one thing does not work, try it another way. These are essential to stop imposing our expectations on our children and help them become avid critical thinkers. They must learn to find solutions on their own. Thinking critically is an undervalued skill, and as parents, it is one of the most, if not the most, crucial skills to have. Critical thinking could make the difference between life and death.

A facilitator shapes the mind to brainstorm, investigate, and solve by asking a series of questions (oh, the 21st-century educator in me!). I want my children to grow up to be good human beings and capable individuals who can think for themselves. We live in a world where foundational morals and values and "upbringing" play a significant role in who children are. Having some expectations is okay, but parents must find the balance between having too many and not enough. An article from Hello Motherhood shared this.

"Parental expectations help nurture your child's sense of self-esteem and encourage healthy development. When expectations are set unrealistically high -- or, on the other hand, ridiculously low -- children's personalities and sense of self-worth are negatively affected. Understanding the outcome and finding a balance is key to promoting healthy development in children."

We never want to do things that will negatively affect our child(ren), but as parents, we also have to realize that we are not perfect and will make mistakes just as our child(ren) will.

We must pay attention to our child(ren) and do what works best for them. We can't worry about what other people think or what other people do for their families. We do what works best for us. It is important to manage our expectations of what they should be versus accepting who they are. They don't need friends. They need accountability, commitment, consistency, and family that is present.

PRAYER:

Father,

I thank you for the precious gift of family. I thank you for the people who have done their best to nurture and care for me. I know they did the best they could with what they had. I will not hold that against them. I'm grateful for my sibling(s) who have been my partners in life's joys and sorrows. I will work to maintain healthy connections with them while also being mindful enough to maintain my boundaries.

Father, thank you for blessing me with a child, children, or young people around me who bring so much joy and love. Father, I will be a positive example in their life and help cultivate the gifts You placed inside of them.

Help me to remember and be mindful of the importance of managing my expectations of family members, as we all have different strengths, weaknesses, and capabilities. Remind us that we should be patient with one another and love one another the same way You love us.

I thank You for the support and love that my family provides, and I ask that you continue to shower us with Your grace and blessings.

Amen.

HOW DO I GET THERE?

ASK: Do I have any unforgiveness in my heart associated explicitly with my family?

BELIEVE: I will be healed in this area and live a life of example.

CONFESS: My relationship with my family will grow stronger, and my children or the children around me will see me as a positive example.

THOUGHTS: _____

_____

_____

How Did I Get Here? It's Not A Question Of Being Lost, But A Question of Being Found.

Chapter 5
The Lord's Prayer

OUR FATHER

Have you ever felt so experienced in an area or on a specific topic that you know it'd be easy to share your knowledge or expertise? You know how it is, you gained all this knowledge, and now you feel like an authority because you've researched it and lived through it. That's exactly how I feel at this very moment as I prepare to share with you about OUR FATHER. Yet, strangely enough, I'm a little nervous as I write about who God—Our Father, is to me. I know who He is, but like many, I'm challenged to find the right words to describe Him.

I've been in the church all of my life. I have a certification in Biblical Studies. I've completed ministry training, pastoral leadership training, and much more. None of this makes me better than the next person and having the knowledge doesn't make describing who Our Father is any easier. However, it does make me pause to reflect. I was reminded that He comforts me in times of trouble. He shows up when others don't and is always with me. When I'm weak, He does some of His best work as He shows Himself to be strong.

Thinking of Him always being with me reminded me that He abides within. Therefore, how I live should reflect the Father-His nature and character. Does my life mirror the Father'? Would others use similar words to describe me that they use to describe Him? These are questions we should all consider. We must realize we may be the only God some people will experience.

Those who encounter me should know that I represent the Kingdom, no matter where I am or what I do. I must admit there have been times when my actions didn't allow the Father to manifest through me. A few times, I had to stop myself from giving place to negative thoughts that tried to destabilize and make me waiver on the dedication and devotion of time given to God and His Kingdom. Nevertheless, I can bring others to Christ by living out my faith. I'm not perfect by any means, but I am intentionally living my life as a reflection of the Kingdom of God.

How I handle life should show that I trust Him, depend on Him and go to Him no matter what's happening around me. So, I'm choosing to live an integral life, one that is holy, acceptable, and pleasing to the Father.

Therefore, I urge you, brothers and sisters, in view of God's mercy, to offer your bodies as a living sacrifice, holy and pleasing to God—this is your true and proper worship.
Romans 12:1 NIV
(copy from bible app)

I know some people may read this and think, "that's a lot of responsibility," but in all honesty, it's an honor to serve and represent the Kingdom of God, showing others who our Father is.

We have enough negative distractions to entice and lure people toward things that bring destruction and bondage. These things pull us out of God's corner and into a place opposite the life God created and ordained us to live. But we must have more people living a life that draws humanity into a place of freedom, love, and intimacy with the Father, a work I take great pride in.

EARTHLY FATHER, HEAVENLY FATHER

When we think about God as our Father, we shouldn't see Him through our experiences with our earthly Fathers, specifically if he failed to be a good one.

Many of us have negative experiences with earthly fathers and allow the dynamic of those relationships to impact how or if we connect with our Spiritual Father. It's important to remember that whatever your earthly Father may or may not have done that has negatively impacted your life does not represent our heavenly Father. How your earthly Father treated or treats you is not the way our heavenly Father treats you. How your earthly Father looks at you, speaks to you, or views you is not how our Spiritual Father sees you.

For I know the plans I have for you,"
declares the LORD, "plans to prosper you
and not to harm you, plans to
give you hope and a future.
Jerimiah 29:11

Scripture reminds us that: We are a chosen generation, a royal priesthood, a holy nation, His own special people, that you may proclaim the praises of Him who called you out of darkness into His marvelous light;(1 Peter 2:9). He sees us a new creation (2 Corinthians 5:17), he sees us as strong and courageous (Joshua 1:9). We must see ourselves as He sees us. Otherwise, we may begin to see ourselves as the world wants us to see ourselves. When we manage our expectations spiritually, we make room to grow and stretch into a place where we can genuinely experience the Father in all His goodness. This allows us to have encounters with Him. An encounter with Jesus always has the power to bring change. When love is present, healing is present. It may not always look miraculous, but it will always make a difference.

Though He is our Father and wants what's best for us, we must keep in mind that He is not a genie in a bottle or a vending machine that exists to give us all we ask for. Instead, he is our loving Savior whose plans for each of our lives are much better than ours. The healing that love brings might not always look like we think it should, but in the scope of eternity, it will prove to be exactly what we need for our good and God's glory.[1]

ARE YOU HERE?

I'm sure we can all think of those moments when we wondered where He was in our time of need or despair. Maybe when we've lost loved ones or had significant trials, we looked around and said, "Okay, I need you to step in right here, God." That would be great, right? However, that's not always the way it works. We must realize that some of the things we do or situations we find ourselves in are because of our choices. I love how my spiritual mentor always says that "where we are is the sum total of the decisions we've made." Everything isn't the devil, and everything isn't someone else's fault. We have to be willing to step up to the plate and accept responsibility for things we've done, the things we've said, and the seeds we've sown. The Father is spending His time trying to make things work out for our good.

He spent His time creating, molding and shaping us. Then, while making us, He spoke life into us. He told us how great we would be and how much He loves us. He laid His hands on every inch of whom we are as beings, speaking life to every part of our bodies. Reminding us that we are created with a purpose. But even though he spent all that time making sure the details of whom we were perfectly aligned, we still had to choose. In moments or seasons of our life where we don't make the best choices, we are still responsible for the consequences of those actions

Many people think that when you get saved, something miraculous happens, and life is automatically better. Some even believe trouble will no longer follow them, but those in a relationship with Him know that's not true. Scripture reminds us that weapons may form, but they won't prosper (Isaiah 54:17). While being saved does give us 100% more life and abundance (John 10:10), we must wake up every day and be intentional about communing with Him so He will continue to direct our path. Though things may try to come against us, it won't matter because we have the Father on our side.

When we make a public confession, asking God to be a part of our life and believing that in our heart, we are saying we know we need to continue to strive toward our goals but need to do them with God. We want to trust Him with our future. Now we want to give Him the merit and the space to help us decide and navigate these situations instead of having to navigate them on our own.

WHEN HAS HE SHOWN UP?

God has saved me so many times I can't even count! Once when I was in high school, my mother let my younger sister and I visit my brother in college. I saw some craziest things staying with my brother those few days. The people around his apartment had parties every night with nonstop drinking and smoking, and the parties looked like so much fun. I went outside and wanted to join in. They had these cute little cups of jello that tasted so good. I figured they were for the younger crowd like me. I was so wrong. They were Jell-O shots. My parents told me about alcohol around age twelve, so I knew what it was, but these Jell-O shots caught me off, guard.

My brother found me and asked, "what are you doing?" It wasn't like he had to look far. I was on his porch. Though he was drinking, he knew it wasn't a good idea for me to do so.

Another time I knew God was watching over us was when we jumped the tracks. We would get in the car, put our seatbelts on and drive as fast as we could, and go so fast over the tracks that our heads would hit the ceiling of the car, and the car would go in the air and hit the ground. While in college, I went places I had no business going. I did things with people who did not have my best interest at heart. I walked away unscathed.

Then, there are more complex situations surrounding domestic violence where God showed His grace and mercy. We can all look back at times when we knew it wasn't us that got us out of certain situations. It was God almighty. Sometimes God allows us to sit in our mess for a while before He rescues us. We think He's abandoned us, but He comes right on time. God's timing and our timing are different. When He knows you're ready for the next move, He will reach deep down and pull us out of darkness and into the light. He will place you back on track to fulfilling the assignment He's given you.

When I am in a close relationship with God, I hear Him differently than when I distance myself. I know some people would like to think that when you "walk with God," you are always seated at His feet, but that's not always the case. Since we are born with a sinful nature (Romans 3:10 ESV, Psalm 51:5 ESV) and the right to choose, we can make some decisions that cause us to stray away from God; of course, He never strays away from us.

"Be strong and courageous. Do not be afraid
or terrified because of them, for the Lord
your God goes with you; he will
never leave you nor forsake you."
Deuteronomy 31:6 (NIV)

Therefore, we can stand firm when we face any situation knowing that our Father is with us.

It can be difficult to describe God's presence with words. He is a subconscious figure who has never left my side. This is actually true when we think about Holy Spirit living in us. I remember times when I would stray from the narrow way, and He subtly reminded me He was still there just so I would turn back to Him in certain seasons of my life. God does things for me in a way that I sometimes can't explain. The way we see God or hear God may look different, but who He is to all of us never changes.

WHAT DO WE BELIEVE?

With millions of people in the world, there are many beliefs represented. What we believe and why we believe it plays a significant role in who we are and how we contribute to society. I shared at the beginning that I grew up around my grandfather, a Baptist preacher, who instilled many morals and values into my family. By the time I was five, I had chosen to give my life to Christ. I remember it like it was yesterday. I had on this red and blue dress with pigtails in my hair. I remember that my grandfather asked if anyone wanted to turn their life over to God and I didn't say a peep. I just looked around to see if anyone else was going to raise their hand. Once service was over, I walked to the front of the church, tugged at my grandfather's robe and looked up at him, and said, "I want to be saved." In his voice of triumph, he said, "Hold on, everyone. My grand-baby wants to give her life to Jesus!" Amen! Everyone shouted. They smiled and clapped and then carried on about their business. Did I really know what I was doing? Not really. I just knew it felt right. These moments were the beginning of my managing expectations of God.

Many of us start to develop a relationship with what we believe at a young age. Drawing close to the way our parents or guardians express their faith. We connect to what we see and hear as a child oftentimes replicating those actions until we become adults and seek knowledge for ourselves. This knowledge either affirms or demolishes what we believe. To manage our expectations of God we have to know who He is. People call Him by many names, but who is He to you? He has proven himself time and time again. All we have to do is go back and look at our lives and see where he's come through, made a way, and shown up for us.

For me, God is my Father, friend, confidant, provider, and protector. He has shown me time and time again that He is not like man. He will do what He said He would and will always be with me. Sometimes that voice of intimidation creeps in and tries to shift my focus, but I know to speak the truth of God's word out loud.[2]

YOUR WILL BE DONE

Too often, we try to depend on what we can do instead of focusing on what God has already done. In Matthew chapter 6, God teaches us how to pray. We must learn how to pray to ensure we are putting ourselves in a position to receive God's blessings. Prayer is a priority.

"Your will be done" is a vital phrase in the Lord's Prayer. Putting ourselves in a position to allow His will to be done means that we will let go and allow Him to act on our behalf. When we do this, we are accessing every element of the Father. He has many names, one of which is Jehovah Jireh which means the Lord, our provider. He's Jehovah Nissi, the Lord my banner, and Jehovah Rapha, the Lord who heals even when we seek healing. Above all names, he is El Shaddai, Lord God Almighty. And when we feel lonely, we must remember that we are never alone because he is Emmanuel God with Us.

God is able and capable of giving us more than we can imagine. Now that we know this think about how you can create a space where you will allow God to do His will and not your own. You have to become intentional about not allowing your flesh, the "inner me"(the thoughts we have), or the enemy (the devil) to get in the way of what God has for us. Letting "His will be done" means obedience to what He has called us to do. God will open doors when we begin to walk in our purpose by being obedient. In Exodus 4, He will often ask us to notice what we have in our own hands rather than giving us something new or different. 2 Peter 1:3 tells us, "His divine power has given us everything we need for a godly life through our knowledge of Him who called us by His own glory and goodness." The truth is, what we need to walk in obedience and accomplish what God has called us to do is not what someone else has but what is within us.

Our dependency upon His power and strength should not fluctuate based on our circumstances. We must be steadfast when we pray and know that it will direct our path. Our praise should stay the same whether things are going well, or we are in the middle of trying times. Our biblical obedience is obedience that should be born out of gratitude, not just duty. Obedience is born out of love! The love for the Father and a humble submission to what He has done for us. Obedience alone, following the "rules" of faith, is not what the believer's life is about.

Living to obey rules won't get us far. Living to love the Lord our God with all our heart, soul, and mind, in loving obedience, will bring us freedom as we have never experienced. It is a promise the Lord makes to His people – that includes you![3]

Many people in the world may make it seem like obedience is difficult, but that's because they place present-day definitions and understandings on these words. It's essential to look back at the biblical definition of obedience and submission to fully understand why the Father desires us to commit to them. Romans 6:16 reminds us that when we choose to obey God, it will lead to righteous Living. I don't know about you, but I want to live a righteous life.

When we learn and understand what it means to obey, we can do it even when it's hard. This allows us to humble ourselves before the Lord and submit to His instruction. Obedience allows us to be more like Jesus, who embraced the change from being infinite as God to finite as man by having a humble attitude, even though he was the Son of God. Instead of asking the Lord to change our circumstances, ask for the Lord to change *us*. Trust that His plan is greater than anything we can fathom.[4] Our plans usually aren't His plans, and obeying means understanding that things may not be done as we think they should be. Just like the official who believed that if Jesus didn't come to his home and heal his son, the boy was sure to die. He pleaded, "Lord, please come now before my little boy dies!" (Vs. 49). He made two common mistakes. He assumed that Jesus had to be present to heal his son and that it would be too late if the boy died! But Jesus showed him that God works a miracle in His time and in His way. So, He tells him, "Go back home. Your son will live!" (Vs. 50). What would you do? This was certainly not what he had expected. Sometimes our expectations of what God should do and how He should do it get in the way of our salvation. You have to give some credit to this official, though. He made no further appeals. As desperate as he was, he chose to believe Jesus and headed home. On the way home, his servants ran to meet him with the good news that his son was alive and well! He discovered the miracle occurred at the exact time Jesus stated, "go back home!"

Another thing that gets in the way of His will is our pride. We must remove prideful behavior and thoughts. "I can do it on my own." Sound familiar? More often than we'd probably like to admit, we rely on our strength to guide us through life. But no part of our life is too small or too big for our Lord! He wants us to rely on Him, not on ourselves. When we pray, we recognize His power and sovereignty over all things.[5] We can expect the Father to rule as He said He would and not lean on our understanding (Proverbs 3:5).

FORGIVE US

Forgiveness can be a touchy topic. As I said earlier in the book, when we talked about learning how to win, we must learn the importance of forgiving ourselves and others. But sometimes, we find ourselves struggling to find forgiveness in our hearts. In the Lord's Prayer, we are reminded to ask for forgiveness and to forgive others. I repeated the Lord's Prayer so much as a child, but the words didn't mean as much to me as they mean now that I understand them. I find myself trying to understand the scriptures to better follow the instructions. When it says, "forgive us," this is what it means. In Matthew 6:14, "you forgive" is 'aphete' in Greek, which means to send forth in various applications.

I had a great conversation with my accountability partner that brought this to light for me. I told her I needed help to stay on track with my eating habits and daily tasks. These were my exact words:

I ate pizza last night. I couldn't resist. It makes me feel terrible. They're two sides to this. (1) why do I lack so much discipline in this area? (2) Am I trying to prove something to God or myself? I have a goal for my appearance. It won't be easy to achieve that without setting some food boundaries. I'm also not preserving my physical health and need to work out. These are just all my thoughts.

She could have taken my words and just responded to me in any kind of way. Still, she asked some clarifying questions to get a deeper understanding. She wrote back, "When you say you feel terrible, do you mean like bloated? Sick? Or do you mean because you ate the food?" My head sank because I knew deep down that I felt terrible just because I had eaten it. She reminded me that adjusting to a new lifestyle takes a while, and it's not about denying myself anything but learning a healthier way to enjoy it. That helped me because I was focused on what not to eat instead of re-searching healthier options to still enjoy the things I like. There was a little more to the story, though. I was reminded that I needed to give myself grace because I thought negatively about myself every time, I ate something I shouldn't. I would ask my-self questions internally like, "Eboni, why are you eating this? Look at you; you don't have any dis-cipline. You want the Father to use you, but you can't follow an instruction you gave yourself?"

It takes time to change a habit, and I had to step up and begin to forgive myself for how I was eating and how I was thinking. I also had to for-give myself for forgetting one crucial detail. God didn't care if I ate the pizza or not. I allowed the enemy to use food to be condemning. She remind-ed me, "the father isn't judging your willingness to say yes or no to Pizza; he's looking at your heart." We place ourselves in choke holds and allow the enemy or "inner me" to win. We must remember it's important to lose things, making forgiving ourselves and others easier.

Any feelings of guilt and images of shame continue to push me in the wrong direction, but every day is a new chance to be a new creation. When we move towards a goal, we're showing self-discipline, and everything is a transferable skill. When we're disciplined with our food, we can be disciplined with our thoughts. When we are disciplined with our thoughts, we can be disciplined with our speech. When we are disciplined in our speech, we can be disciplined in our actions. Discipline is a seed that, when planted, births a harvest in many areas of our life.[6]

The Father loves for us to do the tasks He has assigned us to do because they draw us closer to Him and show Him that we are obedient. Being obedient is a requirement for those living out His word and making space and opportunity for forgiveness to manifest itself in our lives and those around us. It's a part of how we reflect the Kingdom. We have to learn to see ourselves as the Father sees us. He sees us as our Heavenly selves, not as our earthly selves. The more we condemn ourselves, the more we move away from forgiveness. No matter what we do, say, or live, He sees us as our Heavenly selves first, even when we don't forgive ourselves. We should consider ourselves lucky to know that He will take the time to deal with our emotions and human flesh to help us understand the importance of dying to this flesh daily to help fulfill the purpose and the promise that He has designed for us.

> When we are disciplined and able to forgive, it takes us further in our spiritual gifts. IT DOESN'T MOVE THE GIFT; IT MATURES THE GIFT. People who spend time with discipline yield better results.

When we say The Lord's Prayer, we ask the Father to forgive us of our trespasses as we forgive those who trespass against us. We must remember that He's already forgiven us, and we need to receive His forgiveness. We need to learn how to forgive ourselves and forgive others. Walking around with unforgiveness in our hearts can cause us to miss out on so much in this world. We are new creations in Christ with nothing missing or lacking. We have everything we need to operate fully in our purpose and kingdom power.

KINGDOM, POWER & GLORY

Matthew 10:22 enduring to the end is not a way to be saved but evidence that a person is committed to Jesus. Perseverance is not a means to earn salvation; it is the by-product of a truly loving life.

Mark 6:18 shares that believers today face a world of moral compromise and secular power standards corresponding to a majority vote. However, believers' standards begin and end with God's word. To be faithful to God's word, we must stand up against what is morally wrong. Responsible believers must choose their battles. Start with Prayer for wisdom, then prayer for courage. Then speak and act as faithful followers of the Living God; Witness with strength and believe we can move mountains by faith and overcome with love. Show the compromised world a little of John's stubbornness, grit, and faith. Some may wonder, "Who is John the Baptist?" Let me tell you a little about a man who believed in God's Kingdom, submitted to His power, and gave Him all the glory.

John's story is important because it reminds believers how we should live. John was a man many people respected, trusted, and followed because he was faithful to the word of God. King Herod had imprisoned John for many things, but while imprisoned, John told l stories. King Herod would visit his cell to listen to him. Unfortunately, because John kept telling King Herod it was against the law for him to be married to Herodias, the former wife of his brother, Herodias wanted

John dead. However, King Herod, knowing that John was a good and holy man, protected John the Baptist. But one day, Herodias's daughter performed for King Herod during a birthday party. She did so well that he promised with a vow that he would give her anything she wanted. She consulted with her mother and asked for the head of John the Baptist on a tray.

Can you relate to this? Have you ever thought someone cared for you or was protecting you and then found out they were ready to put your head on a tray? They weren't brave enough to stand up for you, to say no when it's needed to defend you. They would instead let you die than step in to speak on your behalf. Though he lost his life, John walked in the truth of God's word. He could have changed his path by succumbing to what people wanted him to say or believe, but he chose to honor God.

We must remember that we are a King's kid, royalty. We have authority and access to the Kingdom, power, and authority, and we need to use it. We can't worry about what other people say or think. We were made to be different. We were made to stand out. We are the salt and the light. So, when people say it's not possible, we say anything is possible with the Father. No one thought

David would be able to defeat Goliath, especially with only a rock and a slingshot, but he did!

> "Don't be ridiculous!" Saul replied. "There's no way you can fight this Philistine and possibly win! You're only a boy, and he's been a man of war since his youth."
> 1 Samuel 17:33 NLT

David knew he wasn't going in alone. It was his own family who doubted him. They wanted him to think that he would fail. The only thing worse than asking yourself, "What if I fail?" is someone confirming your fear and telling you that you will fail. Unlike the voice of limitation, which tells you that you can't do it, or the voice of manipulation, which tells you that you don't have what it takes, the voice of intimidation tells you that you will not succeed. David knew that he had what it took. He knew what he had done to lions and bears before. David knew that God had rescued him and would rescue him again. He did it his way, not using the typical armor but using what God gave him, a slingshot. He knew he could do it with the power of God. That rock and sling-shot did more than kill a philistine, it deepened the faith of those around him, and God was given all the glory.

There's a quote from Jenny Simmons in her book The Road to Becoming that says, "I'm learning to live without a map which is good because the road to becoming is map-less. All I need is a guide who knows the way to the other side." For me, the guide has been and will continue to be God. I got here by being found in His presence. I'm so grateful to have Him on this journey with me.

PRAYER

Father, I'm so grateful for the relationship I have with you. I will not place any earthly expectations on my heavenly God. I will not allow my relationship with my earthly father to impact my expectations of my Heavenly Father. I acknowledge that You already have plans for me and that I will stay out of my own way so they can manifest. I know that You will show up for me. I know that I can trust You. I know that You will never leave me nor forsake me. I appreciate all You have done, all You are doing, and all that You will do. You are a promise keeper.

Amen!

HOW DO I GET THERE?

ASK: How is it that I desire to be in a relationship with the Father?

BELIEVE: He desires to be in a close relationship with me.

CONFESS: I am worthy of His love.

THOUGHTS: _____

_____

_____

_____

_____

_____

_____

_____

_____

_____

_____

_____

_____

_____

_____

_____

_____

_____

_____

_____

_____

Extra Thoughts

DOING THINGS IN EXCELLENCE

The work of showing people the importance or value of doing things in intimacy with Father and doing it with excellence is an honor and an intricate part of my daily life.

As previously shared, at the time of writing, my children are 3, 7, and 8, and excellence is often discussed in our home. When they want to do what other children do, I remind them of the presence of excellence within them, and when we do things with what we have, we always represent the Kingdom.

When people see me, I want them to see the excellence of the Kingdom and how worthy my heavenly Father is.

Human hearts are not changed or set free by earthly things. Only God and His Word can change hearts. Even when obeying the Bible can sometimes be challenging or uncomfortable, it will set you free. The Bible tells you how you can be saved. It tells you that your life isn't an accident. The Bible tells you how to be forgiven. It tells you how God can use you for good in the world.[7]

"Don't let anyone think less of you because you are young. Be an example to all believers in what you say, in the way you live, in your love, your faith, and your purity. Until I get there, focus on reading the Scriptures to the church, encouraging the believers, and teaching them."

ENDNOTES

1   Devotion Day 6, Dave Willis The Seven Laws of Love

2   Natalie Grant & Charlette Gimble, walking in obedience devotion day 4

3   Chad Johnson of Compassion International Obedience to the Lord in the Midst of Challenges Devotion Day 4

4   Chuck Rosinski of Compassion International, Obedience to the Lord in the midst of Change Devotion Day 7

5   Jennifer Cunningham of Compassion International Obedience to the Lord in the Midst of Challenges Devotion Day 3

6   Conversation with an accountability partner, audio message.

7   YouVersion Devotion: Renewed, Restored, Day 20

ABOUT THE AUTHOR

Eboni Walker is an empowerment specialist, revolutionary thinker, and transformational leader. As a veteran of the military and her faith, she has earned a reputation as a prayer warrior, compassionate believer, free worshiper, impactful leader, and lover of all whom God created. Eboni believes that God is at the core of everything we do, which is why she also uses her gift as a faith-based speaker, coach, and mentor.

Seasoned with humor, compassion, truth, and power, Eboni brings clarity and understanding through God's word, empowering individuals to activate purpose and maximize potential. She frequently appears in national prayer circles, panels, magazine articles, events, and keynotes on national platforms touching many with the Gospel.

Eboni's three key areas are power in prayer, truth in the word, and restoration of the soul and mind. Her goal is to equip, encourage and empower minds to go forward and change the world.

Eboni believes in giving back to her community and cultivating the gifts in those around her

Website: EboniWalker.com

YouTube page:
https://youtube.com/@EboniWalker

Facebook: Eboni Walker

Instagram: @itsmrswalker

Email: E.walker@eboniwalker.com

Made in the USA
Columbia, SC
22 March 2023